Climbing Walls

a complete guide

JIM STIEHL, PhD
TIM B. RAMSEY, MA

University of Northern Colorado

HUMAN KINETICS

Library of Congress Cataloging-in-Publication Data

Stiehl, Jim.
  Climbing walls : a complete guide / Jim Stiehl, Tim B. Ramsey.
    p. cm.
  Includes bibliographical references and index.
  ISBN 0-7360-4831-6 (soft cover)
  1. Rock climbing. I. Ramsey, Tim B., 1950- II. Title.
  GV200.2.S75 2005
  796.52'23--dc22

                                    2004009348

ISBN: 0-7360-4831-6

The Web addresses cited in this text were current as of August 2004, unless otherwise noted.

Acquisitions Editor: Gayle Kassing, PhD; **Developmental Editor:** R. Chris Johns; **Assistant Editor:** Derek Campbell; **Copyeditor:** Pat Connolly; **Proofreader:** Kim Thoren; **Indexer:** Sharon Duffy; **Permission Manager:** Dalene Reeder; **Graphic Designer:** Robert Reuther; **Graphic Artist:** Dawn Sills; **Photo Manager:** Kareema McLendon; **Cover Designer:** Keith Blomberg; **Photographer (front cover):** © Gopher Sport; **Photographer (back cover):** © Nicros; **Photographer (interior):** Kelly J. Huff, except where otherwise noted. Figure 3.6 © Dianna Gray; figure 4.4 © Jim Stiehl; **Art Manager:** Kelly Hendren; **Illustrators:** Argosy (pp. 28 and 46) and Keri Evans (pp. 95 and 96); **Printer:** Versa Press

We thank the Upper Limits Rock Gym in Bloomington, Illinois, for assistance in providing the location for the photo shoot for this book.

Printed in the United States of America   10   9   8   7   6   5   4   3   2   1

Human Kinetics
Web site: www.HumanKinetics.com

United States: Human Kinetics
P.O. Box 5076
Champaign, IL 61825-5076
800-747-4457
e-mail: humank@hkusa.com

Canada: Human Kinetics
475 Devonshire Road Unit 100
Windsor, ON N8Y 2L5
800-465-7301 (in Canada only)
e-mail: orders@hkcanada.com

Europe: Human Kinetics
107 Bradford Road
Stanningley
Leeds LS28 6AT, United Kingdom
+44 (0) 113 255 5665
e-mail: hk@hkeurope.com

Australia: Human Kinetics
57A Price Avenue
Lower Mitcham, South Australia 5062
08 8277 1555
e-mail: liaw@hkaustralia.com

New Zealand: Human Kinetics
Division of Sports Distributors NZ Ltd.
P.O. Box 300 226 Albany
North Shore City
Auckland
0064 9 448 1207
e-mail: blairc@hknewz.com

contents

1 Introduction to Climbing 1

2 Designing a Climbing Wall 9

3 Constructing a Climbing Wall 43

preface

Over the past few years, interest in climbing has reached new heights—so to speak. Observing Sylvester Stallone dangling over a steep abyss in the movie *Cliffhanger,* or following the exploits of the mighty Lynn Hill, the first person to complete a free ascent of "The Nose" route on Yosemite's famous El Capitan, you might assume that climbing is the sole province of strong, brave, and perhaps somewhat foolish athletes.

But all of us are natural climbers. As soon as we learn to walk, we try to climb anything and everything: chairs, stairs, ladders, trees, and fences. Now, with the increased availability of artificial climbing walls in gyms and recreation centers around the country, enjoyable climbing experiences can be provided to novices and veterans, kids and adults, and fit and not-so-fit individuals.

Once deemed a fringe, extreme sport, climbing has evolved into a fun-filled activity, an educational medium, and a continually growing sport that attracts preschoolers through senior citizens. In all regions of the country, climbing walls are appearing in schools, at camps, on university and college campuses, in health clubs and community centers, and even in retail stores. In attempts to convert existing structures into climbing walls, some inspired individuals have even bolted artificial holds onto silos, office buildings, and bridges. And although beyond the scope of this book, there are commercial gyms designed exclusively for climbing. Some of these gyms include enormous freestanding boulders, caves, and structures that replicate real rocks from famous climbing areas around the world.

Clearly, climbing walls have become popular in schools, universities, recreation centers, camps, and other settings. According to the Sporting Goods Manufacturers Association, climbing on artificial walls has increased by 27 percent since the year 2000. It is one of the fastest developing activities. Some climbing facilities are geared toward developing fitness or preparing a person for climbing outdoors. Some are designed as part of a challenge course. Others place emphasis on fun and the thrill of climbing. Since climbing activities foster enjoyment and self-satisfaction, climbing appeals to a variety of participants—not just athletes.

Climbing Walls: A Complete Guide is a resource for those of you who are already involved with climbing walls, and for those who might be thinking about doing so. We have designed this book to support those who supervise or provide instruction on a wall, as well as for anyone planning to construct or expand an existing wall or program. As mentioned earlier, the nuances and complexities of commercial climbing gyms are beyond the scope and intent of this book. Furthermore, some walls now include opportunities for lead climbs; that is, ascending a wall using intermediate anchors instead of the benefit of a solid anchor system at the top of a climb. This type of climbing involves much more risk and skill than most supervisors and instructors care to include. Thus, our comments about lead climbing are not extensive, but are included where basic knowledge could be useful for safety and instructional purposes (especially if you inherit a climbing wall with lead routes). Nonetheless, our emphasis is on bouldering (climbing close to the ground without anchors, ropes, and harnesses) and top-roping (using a rope and anchoring system for higher climbs that, in the event of a fall, could result in serious injury or worse).

In any wall climbing program, safety is paramount. Whereas the perceived risks associated with climbing can impart excitement and adventure among participants, the potential actual risks can be a major source of anxiety among administrators and instructors. In an effort to preserve the excitement associated with perceived risks while simultaneously avoiding real hazards, we will identify potential risks and how to address them so that you can be vigilant in creating a challenging yet safeguarded environment for your clientele.

This book is organized into six chapters. Following an introductory chapter, chapters 2, 3, and 4 address design, construction, and equipment considerations. Chapters 5 and 6 provide basic operating guidelines and activities.

Chapter 1: Introduction to Climbing. Following some introductory comments about climbing walls, this chapter emphasizes the goals and benefits that participants can achieve.

Chapter 2: Designing a Climbing Wall. This chapter examines essential considerations during the planning phase for a climbing wall. Included are examples of the wide spectrum of wall designs and features (e.g., overhangs, lead climb protection anchors, characteristics of holds) along with information to assist individuals in seeking answers to specific design questions and problems.

Chapter 3: Constructing a Climbing Wall. In addition to describing procedures for constructing various types of walls, this chapter presents factors to consider such as industry standards and local specifications and codes. Also included are discussions of contractor skills and experience, liability coverage, and factors affecting costs.

Chapter 4: Selecting Climbing Equipment. In this chapter, besides pointing out technical aspects of each piece of equipment, there is discussion of how the equipment functions with other equipment and the climbing structure. Included are suggestions for documenting use of ropes, harnesses, carabiners, and other common types of equipment.

Chapter 5: Developing and Managing a Climbing Program. Ensuring that staff will supervise effectively and provide sound, meaningful experiences for participants is the next step. This chapter covers information about basic operating guidelines and general emergency procedures. It also includes a discussion of standards for administrators, staff, and participants as well as how program staff can assist in serving the needs of a diverse clientele. The chapter ends with an explanation of the basic skills needed by participants before they can actually begin climbing.

Chapter 6: Climbing Activities and Games. This chapter provides a variety of climbing activities for participants with a wide range of abilities and interests. From specific activities to games that build upon concepts in *Changing Kids' Games* (Morris and Stiehl 1999), the chapter offers strategies for staff and participants to discover and invent endless variations of games and activities for climbing walls.

Appendixes provide further information: In appendix A, you will find climbing wall program forms that an instructor and administrator can use for risk management and operation of the climbing wall. In appendix B, we list sources and resources for additional information on topics such as liability, equipment, and construction.

Advocates claim that climbing strengthens the body, challenges the mind, and uplifts the spirit. *Climbing Walls: A Complete Guide* presents the complete guide for everyday use in school, recreation, camp, and community settings so that instructors and administrators can provide a healthy, fun activity in which everyone can participate.

acknowledgments

Prior to writing this book together, our paths were quite different. But converging paths permitted us to climb and work side-by-side. Our acknowledgments, therefore, are mutual and separate.

Together we thank our colleagues and staff at the University of Northern Colorado for allowing us to practice what we preach—that is, climbing can be a fun, educational activity for everyone (or in their words, "And you guys get paid to do this?"). Also Nate Postma of the Climbing Wall Association deserves our deep gratitude. He has kept us abreast of the climbing industry's most up-to-date thinking. This is a challenging task in the rapidly changing world of climbing. Finally, we appreciate the untiring support of the Human Kinetics staff, particularly Gayle Kassing, Chris Johns, and Derek Campbell who, in each communication with us, conveyed a genuine interest in every aspect of climbing which, in turn, inspired us to work and climb harder.

Jim expresses gratitude to his friend and colleague, Jeff Steffen, for introducing him to the joys of *calculated* risk-taking ("there's old climbers, and bold climbers; but no old bold climbers") and for laying the foundation for the continuing outdoor and adventure programs at UNC. He also thanks another long-time friend and colleague, Cheryl Kent, who was the driving force in acquiring UNC's climbing wall. She has refuted those naysayers who once declared it "just a fad." Finally, thanks to those many school and community partners who have supported kids' growth through climbing.

Tim wishes to thank his parents for introducing him to the world of nature and outdoor pursuits, out of which recreational and professional experiences grew. He also thanks his long-time climbing partner, Pete Helmetag, for sharing their many adventures in rock climbing and the mountain world; and his friend and colleague, Steve Roberts, Director of the Slippery Rock University Outdoor Adventures Program, for his unfailing willingness to share professional information and outdoor adventures. Special thanks goes to all the students of Tim's rock climbing classes whose enthusiasm for learning to climb keeps him involved in the educational and recreational joys of climbing. Most importantly, deepest thanks go to Jim (his co-author) for taking up the writing slack and guiding Tim along the writing path when he ventured into the more familiar and comfortable world of the outdoors.

As a final point, we thank publicly our respective companions, Julie Trujillo and Missy Parker. While not accompanying us on every climbing foray, they at least indulge the two of us in our need to visit the backcountry together (and we're afraid to ask what they do while we're gone).

a note about safety

Despite all of the technological advances in artificial wall climbing during recent years, climbing is still an inherently dangerous activity involving risk of serious injury or even death. Though indoor climbers are not susceptible to many of the hazards that may be present in outdoor rock climbing (e.g., weather, falling rocks, poison ivy, wasps, and rattlesnakes), indoor climbing still presents potential dangers. Among these are loose or damaged holds; falling to the ground or onto other participants; abrasions from walls, ropes, or the floor; equipment failure or belay failure; or climbing out of control or beyond one's personal limits.

Critical to minimizing such risks is education, and this book provides a reasonable starting point. However, you should not depend solely on information gleaned from this book for safety. No document can address the particulars of every situation. Facility operators and instructors must remember that their best judgment and discretionary actions may differ from what is written in this book. Moreover, there is no substitute for personal instruction when it comes to learning climbing safety techniques and operational practices. If you misinterpret a concept expressed in this book, someone may be seriously injured as a result of the misunderstanding. Therefore, the information provided in this book should be used only to supplement competent instruction and guidance from qualified and experienced climbing instructors and climbing facility operators. Even as you become proficient in climbing safety, occasional use of a climbing instructor is a recommended way to raise your climbing standards and to acquire advanced information about accepted industry practices.

In summary, artificial wall climbing can never be guaranteed as safe. However, maintaining a reasonable margin of safety can minimize the inherent dangers. With proper education and adherence to accepted risk management and operational practices, indoor climbing can be relatively safe for persons of all ages.

Introduction to Climbing

66 A climbing wall is not just a one-shot carnival ride with a fifty-dollar bill taped to the top of it. 99

Michael Popke (2003)

Over the past two decades, interest in climbing has gone "sky high," as has the proliferation of commercial companies that manufacture climbing walls and equipment. Climbing walls have become ingrained into the fitness and recreation culture. On college campuses, climbing is being introduced to new legions of participants. Many public schools are now incorporating climbing walls into their physical education programs. Indeed, the federal government, through its Physical Education Program (PEP) bill, recommends a traverse climbing wall as one of the pieces of equipment that can be used to help initiate, expand, and improve physical education programs for kindergarten through grade 12 students. Corporate groups often make climbing walls one component of leadership training. Hosting climbing competitions, throwing birthday parties, creating a training environment for local climbers preparing for a major ascent, and providing athletic opportunities for youngsters (climbing's next generation) who might not otherwise participate in organized sports are all becoming commonplace at climbing walls.

So what accounts for the skyrocketing popularity of climbing walls? For starters, they're conspicuous if not striking. Today's climbing walls are far more varied and beautiful than those of just a few years ago. There are self-paced, rotating walls; climbing towers with rocklike texture; custom walls featuring cracks and lead routes; innovative playground climbing structures; racquetball court conversions; and portable, durable walls

Climbing's rising popularity can be attributed, in part, to the outstanding design and construction of today's climbing walls.

and towers that can be hauled on custom trailers to various locations. People sometimes know about a particular school, recreation center, or health club because of its climbing wall. The wall serves as a landmark and generates interest not only in climbing but in other activities at that site as well.

Climbing walls also have the advantage of being wonderfully versatile. For those people who have spent years getting fit and are bored with old machines, climbing walls can always present new challenges. Climbing holds can be repositioned to create a potentially unlimited variety of climbing routes. For example, easy routes placed adjacent to more challenging routes will attract beginners and increase their confidence. Similarly, color coding all the holds on a single route allows climbers with different skill levels to use the same route yet choose different holds. Thus, by varying the difficulty of various routes, a wide range of climbers can be served on a single wall—all of this occurring in a controlled environment.

Health and Social Benefits

Another advantage of a climbing wall is that it provides health benefits and cross-training potential. Wall climbing frequently becomes an alternative to more common indoor physical activities or, perhaps better, becomes a cross-training exercise that is balanced with other activities. Recognizing the health benefits of climbing, many programs couple their climbing technique classes with clinics on stretching, diet, avoiding overuse injuries, and weight training.

Specific physical benefits of climbing include (1) enhanced fine motor skills; (2) strengthened back, leg, shoulder, and forearm muscles; and (3) increased endurance and flexibility. But climbing a wall is a mental and emotional as well as a physical experience. Selecting an appropriate climbing route while undergoing physical exertion requires strategies and imagination. Many people who have never tried indoor climbing mistakenly believe that its primary prerequisite is extraordinary upper body strength. When climbing, however, technique is more important than strength—this is a pleasant surprise to the novice climber. Women in particular often become enamored with climbing when they realize that their performance will improve without even working on power and endurance. Other important aspects of climbing include footwork, coordination, balance, and concentration—all forms of positive power. Nonetheless, if someone is already in good physical condition, climbing is an excellent cross-training activity that promotes strength, endurance, body control, and precision of movement.

Benefits to Schools

In public schools, climbing activities have been used to make physical education more attractive. Some of today's youngsters, raised on the fast-paced entertainment of video games and television, find physical activity tedious or even humiliating. Some team sports discourage those who have the most to gain from physical activity. And an overdose of jumping jacks, sit-ups, and stretching routines can be boring even to the most enthused student. But boredom and embarrassment are seldom seen on the faces of kids who, like little sand crabs and with support from a classmate ("spotter"), stretch and grasp their way across appropriately challenging climbing routes.

In public schools, climbing walls can also be used as one way of addressing national physical education goals. For instance, climbing requires interpersonal skills (cooperation, communication, and sometimes conflict resolution), cognitive skills (planning, decision making, and problem solving), and physical skills (balance, coordination, strength, and flexibility). Climbing success can also enhance self-esteem, self-confidence, patience, perseverance, and courage. Thus, physical education teachers are teaching climbing alongside other less traditional activities (e.g., in-line skating) as well as traditional physical education units.

Other proponents of climbing walls call attention to the personal and social benefits of climbing: camaraderie, confidence, teamwork, trust, cooperation, pushing a person's limits to the maximum without significant danger, and, of course, fun and the inherent pleasure that climbing brings. Consider the following examples of climbing walls and their many advantages.

> The Boston Children's Museum reached new heights by adding a climbing wall exhibit. The wall is intended to challenge youngsters' physical and mental abilities, as well as those of adults.

> In Williamston, Michigan, the PTA bought a climbing wall for students at two elementary schools. Teachers assert that it will promote more than strength, flexibility, and confidence. Their goal is to weave the climbing wall into their curriculum, because it will develop team-building, leadership, and communication skills.

> Scaling Mount Zot at the campus recreation center of the University of California at Irvine, university students step out of their comfort zone. Many students climb for the challenge of it, stress relief, and the mental benefits, as well as for fun.

> Throughout the nation, schools, universities, and communities are working together to plan and fund climbing walls that will open their doors to students while providing access to community residents. The new $12 million fitness center addition at Lake Shore Senior High School in Evans, New York, features a climbing wall. Williams University's climbing wall offers activities to the students and is part of an outreach program to the community.

Climbing activities make physical education more fun, and they help develop students' physical and social skills.
© Gopher Sport

Rock-climbing walls installed at several Arlington, Virginia, elementary schools are longer than they are tall—8 feet (2.4 meters) high and 32 feet (9.7 meters) long—so the children move mostly across rather than up and don't need a safety harness. Not only have the climbing walls made exercise more attractive, but they are so "in" that the students' older siblings even go to rock-climbing classes on dates.

Cost, Space, and Safety

Despite the popularity of climbing activities, several potential disadvantages have prevented the construction of climbing walls: cost to build, availability of wall space, and risk management. Although the construction of some climbing walls can be an expensive undertaking, the costs of adding a climbing wall to existing facilities can be as low as $600, which is less than the cost of much playground equipment. Furthermore, climbing walls may be used year-round, and they provide the capacity for an ever-changing environment due to the boundless options for arranging the placement of holds. The size and complexity of a wall will determine its cost, and the primary consideration is to make sure that any wall is safe and reliable.

Although availability of wall space can be a consideration, it need not be a significant barrier. An average top-rope wall can be built in the space of a racquetball court and can provide roughly 2,200 square feet (204 square meters) of climbable space on three walls—20 feet (6 meters) tall, 40 linear feet (12 meters) of climbing wall. Individual panels, configured as slabs or modules, can be purchased ready-made to fit almost any indoor space. These slabs come with a variety of relief (contours and raised surfaces) and removable holds. On the other hand, most public school gymnasiums can accommodate a smaller—8 feet (2.4 meters) high and 32 feet (9.7 meters) long—bouldering or traverse climbing wall. Plywood panels can be used to construct this type of wall; and, to provide various challenges, each panel can be designed to be more difficult than the last.

In our litigious society, risk management is always a valid concern. Safety is paramount. On the one hand, many people erroneously view climbing as exceedingly dangerous. They have a preconceived notion that it is a thrill seeker's sport and, therefore, they do not appreciate the fact that the risk involved with indoor walls is substantially controllable. If everyone involved follows reasonable safety and management guidelines, climbing is a sport where most people can enjoy success. They can push their limits without significant danger.

On the other hand, climbing is an activity not to be taken lightly. It presents potential hazards involving risk of serious injury or even death. Among these are loose or damaged holds; falling to the ground or onto other participants; abrasions from walls, ropes, or the floor; equipment failure or belay failure; and climbing out of control or beyond an individual's personal limits. These and other potential risks establish, for some, the sport's attractiveness. Nevertheless, maintaining a reasonable margin of safety can minimize the inherent dangers. With good-quality facilities, proper education, and adherence to accepted risk management and operational practices, indoor climbing can be relatively safe for persons of all ages and abilities. We will cover important safety issues in more depth later in this book.

In our view, the advantages of climbing walls strongly outweigh any potential disadvantages. As a physical activity and sport, climbing meets different needs for diverse groups by providing

- an outlet for children to focus their natural disposition to climb,
- experiences of genuine success for able and less-able individuals,
- an exciting option for improving fitness among students in public school and extended-day programs,
- a physical and mental challenge (and stress reliever) for college students as part of campus recreation activities,

- a means for promoting teamwork and leadership in corporate training sessions, and
- a fun leisure activity for the entire family.

Summary

In schools, universities, camps, recreation centers, health clubs, and community and business settings, climbing walls have proliferated. In addition to the benefits already mentioned, some people tout the advantages of artificial climbing environments over outdoor settings. First, as rock climbing continues to grow in popularity, climbing walls may provide an alternative to excursions into natural settings. Second, climbing walls provide opportunities not available to those people living in areas where rock-climbing sites are either nonexistent or crowded. Last, many climbing walls allow climbers the freedom to experience holds, cracks, dihedrals, overhangs, and other features of outdoor rock climbing, but in a climate-controlled, indoor facility. Where else can a person climb on a snowy winter night wearing only a tank top and shorts?

2

Designing a Climbing Wall

You have decided that a climbing wall is worth pursuing for your program. Now it is time to start planning what kind of climbing wall design will meet your program and participant needs and objectives. As you enter the planning and design phase, make sure you have a clear understanding of the potential benefits, what your objectives for the wall's use are, who your participants will be, and why the participants will be using your wall. You want to spend quality research and development time at this stage to produce a climbing wall that will be aesthetic, structurally sound, within your financial abilities, and highly functional for your program and participants. You also want to get the most features for your money, while not incorporating climbing wall features that you cannot or will not use once in operation.

At the beginning of the planning and design phase, you should talk with professional climbing wall manufacturers, builders, designers, or engineers who are members of recognized professional climbing wall industry associations. These professionals can inform you of the variety of design features, engineering considerations, and wall construction methods that may best fit your objectives and needs as well as your site. (Refer to appendix B for specific contact information on provided resources.) In the United States, look for professionals who are members of the Climbing Wall Association (CWA), a nonprofit association consisting of climbing gym owners, wall manufacturers, wall builders, and other climbing wall industry participants. In the recent past, two now-disbanded subgroups of the Outdoor Industry Association—the Climbing Wall Industry Group (CWIG) and the Climbing Gym Association (CGA)—provided (CWIG) and executed (CGA) the voluntary climbing wall design and construction standards used in the United States. Currently, these CWIG standards still serve as the recognized minimal U.S. voluntary standards for artificial climbing wall design, engineering, and construction. Some locales may require additional local standards. If your climbing wall will be located outside of the United States, you should consult with members of the professional climbing wall manufacturers, builders, or designers association under whose purview your locale falls. The Climbing Wall Manufacturers Association (CWMA) and the Comité Européen de Normalisation (CEN), based in Europe, are two well-known professional associations implementing climbing wall standards overseas. In addition to using the services of climbing wall professionals, you can use this chapter as a guide for making informed fundamental climbing wall design and construction choices.

Types of Climbing

To make knowledgeable climbing wall design decisions, you need a basic understanding of the various types of climbing. Climbing on artificial climbing walls tends to occur in three basic forms: bouldering, top-roping, and lead climbing. Bouldering and top-roping are by far the most common climbing activities at most climbing walls.

Bouldering

Bouldering, sometimes referred to as traversing, is a form of climbing that emphasizes practicing climbing moves and performing physical training close to the ground, rather than having to get to the top of the wall (figure 2.1). Movement often occurs in the horizontal plane as well as in the vertical plane. Vertical climbing is limited to relatively short distances above the landing surface. Ten to 14 feet (3.0 to 4.2 meters) is often cited as the maximum height above the landing surface, but the distance may need to be lower for special bouldering situations, such as bouldering on the ceiling of an overhanging feature, or for participant considerations, such as age or skill level. Belay (safety) ropes are not used in bouldering. Instead, trained spotters are used to help protect a falling boulderer. A spotter is someone who is trained to stand behind a boulderer on the wall and who

FIGURE 2.1   Bouldering.

physically helps to protect a falling boulderer from landing badly on the landing surface. Refer to "Spotting" in chapter 5 (page 93) for a more complete discussion. Spotting is particularly important when a boulderer is climbing in a leaning back position.

Top-Roping

Top-roping is a form of climbing in which the climber wears a harness that has a belay rope attached to it. When the climber is standing on the ground, the belay rope runs upward from the climber, over or through

FIGURE 2.2   Top-roping.
© Nicros

FIGURE 2.3   A trained belayer uses proper belaying techniques and equipment to arrest a climber's fall.

a top-rope running anchor located at the top of the route being climbed, and then back down to a belayer standing on the ground near the climber (figure 2.2).

As the climber ascends vertically, the belayer takes in rope slack, keeping the belay rope gently snug on the ascending climber without actually supporting the climber's weight as she climbs. In the event of a fall, the belayer arrests the falling climber's drop by preventing the rope from sliding back over or through the top-rope running anchor. Commonly, a bight, or bend of rope, is passed through a belay device and then clipped into a locking carabiner that secures it to the belayer's harness. This device, when used properly, can provide enough friction to enable a trained belayer to arrest a falling climber's fall (figure 2.3).

Top-rope climbing is done in the vertical plane, and when done in conjunction with proper belaying techniques, it can allow a climber to climb higher heights with minimal risk. Good top-rope climbing technique requires that the climber stay more or less in line vertically with the top-rope running anchor as he climbs. This will prevent potentially hazardous pendulum (swinging) falls, which add to the potential for injury from hitting features on the wall or climbers on adjacent routes. This is particularly important the closer the climber gets to the top-rope running anchor, because it lessens the possibility of an increased vertical drop by the climber before he can pendulum quickly across the face of the wall. Additionally, good top-roping technique requires that the climber not climb above the top-rope running anchor in most climbing wall situations. To do so would put the climber into a lead-climbing fall situation.

Lead Climbing

Lead climbing on a climbing wall requires a series of protection anchors (to which quickdraws are attached) vertically spaced at proper intervals going up the wall (figure 2.4). The ascending lead climber will clip her belay rope into the nonlocking carabiner of each protection anchor quickdraw as she reaches each protection anchor, in order of ascent. This process continues until the lead climber reaches the top of the route, where special top anchors or top-rope running anchors are located to which she attaches her belay rope in preparation to be lowered back down to the ground by the belayer. The belay rope, which is attached to the climber's harness, runs down through the protection anchor pieces to the belayer standing on the floor at the base of the route being climbed. The belayer may or may not be anchored to a floor anchor, depending on the situation.

Because the climber is climbing above the last protection anchor she has clipped the rope to, a fall will cause her to fall twice the distance she is above the last clip-in point before the belay rope will begin to arrest her fall, when properly belayed (figure 2.5).

Under normal conditions, this kind of fall generates much greater forces for the belayer, the climbing wall structure, and the anchors to deal with as compared to top-roping falls. The distance of a fall in top-roping before the belay rope begins to arrest the climber's fall is equal to the amount of slack in the

FIGURE 2.4   Lead climbing.

FIGURE 2.5   A lead climber will fall twice the distance from the last clip-in point before the rope arrests the fall.

belay rope between the belayer and the climber at the time of the fall. If the belayer is doing his job of keeping the amount of slack in the rope to a minimum ("gently snug" on the climber), then the fall will be short. In lead climbing, the potential hazards of a fall are also increased, when compared to well-belayed top-roping falls, because of the longer falling distances associated with lead climbing. These additional risk management factors, along with the extra expense for building lead-climbing-capable walls, are primary reasons many climbing wall programs have not included lead climbing in their climbing wall designs and construction.

Types of Climbing Walls

Climbing walls come in all shapes and sizes and are designed for a variety of intended uses. However, they tend to fall into two basic categories: bouldering walls and tall walls.

Bouldering Walls

Bouldering is the only form of climbing that takes place on a bouldering wall. The maximum height of a bouldering wall is usually around 10 to 14 feet (3.0 to 4.2 meters), though certain design features such as an overhang may require lower heights due to safety concerns. Bouldering walls designed for young children are often of lower maximum height as well. Bouldering walls come in a plethora of configurations, including simple flat vertical traversing walls; portable traversing walls; walls with corners and edges, highly convoluted surfaces, or overhangs; stand-alone bouldering islands; bouldering caves; or a combination of types (figure 2.6).

A special landing surface should be used under all climbing areas. Bouldering walls are good for practicing basic and advanced climbing movement techniques without the need for belay ropes, and they are very useful for physical training specific to climbing. Spotting should be employed for all bouldering activities.

Bouldering walls tend to be lower in cost, may require less room (depending on design), and allow a greater number of

FIGURE 2.6   Self-standing bouldering islands.
© Nicros

FIGURE 2.7 **Bouldering wall for children.**
© Gopher Sport

active climbers at one time. Lower height, vertically oriented traversing walls, whether of simple flat design or having inside corners and outside edges, are suitable for younger children (figure 2.7).

On traversing walls for younger children, a brightly colored horizontal line is often placed on the wall one to two feet (30 to 60 centimeters) above the landing surface. This line serves as a visual reminder of how high the children are allowed to go on the wall—the bouldering child may not have his feet any higher than the line. Bouldering walls for adults and older children need a greater variety of features and heights to help maintain the climbers' interest in using the wall and to increase the wall's value as a training aid. Bouldering usually takes place both in a traversing manner and in short vertical routes often of higher difficulty.

Tall Walls

Tall walls are generally constructed to a height of 20 to 36 feet (6 to 10 meters), but they can be much higher if the space and money available to build the wall allow. The taller the wall, the more money it will cost in general. But building walls over 36 feet greatly increases the cost of the wall because of the extra expense for having to use larger scissors lifts and other construction equipment than is required for walls less than 36 feet in height. Tall walls require the use of belay ropes and associated anchors and equipment to help safeguard vertically ascending climbers. The belay ropes are also used to lower the climbers back down to the landing surface either when the climber has gotten to the top of the climb or when

FIGURE 2.8   Tall wall.
© Nicros

she becomes unable to continue to climb upward. All tall walls require suitable landing surfaces under all climbing areas. Many programs include appropriately placed floor anchors for belayers to hook into as they belay the climbing routes of a tall wall.

Tall walls tend to be multipurpose climbing facilities (figure 2.8). They are most often used for top-roping, but some are also designed and equipped to allow lead-climbing activities. Bouldering capabilities are usually designed into the lower portion of tall walls; however, some climbing wall programs prefer to have separate locations for bouldering and tall wall activities (i.e., top-roping and lead climbing) as part of the same facility, but this adds considerably to the overall costs of construction. For obvious reasons, boulderers should not climb directly under someone who is top-roping or lead climbing a tall wall route. This applies to two boulderers or two tall wall climbers as well. Many tall walls have a brightly colored horizontal line on the lower portion of the wall to indicate the height above which either the boulderer's hands or feet may not go. The decision to include lead-climbing capabilities in a tall wall's design and construction needs to be based on your program goals, needs, and objectives; on the clientele to be served; and on operation and money considerations.

Tall walls designed to accommodate lead climbing are more expensive to build, require additional training of staff and participants, and often present greater risk management considerations and insurance expenses. Programs looking to focus on the rock-climbing community or intending to help indoor climbers transition to sport climbing outdoors on natural rock may want to consider lead-climbing capabilities for their tall wall. But you must be aware that the knowledge and skills necessary for climbing indoors are not sufficient for climbing on outdoor natural rock formations. Indoor climbers should get additional instruction on climbing natural rock outdoors before doing so. For most educational and introductory level recreational climbing programs, the extra costs associated with the construction and equipment for lead-climbing capabilities on a tall wall may not be worth it, because they are rarely used for the clientele served.

Design Considerations

Good bouldering walls and tall walls come in many different shapes and sizes, are designed for a variety of uses, and are built using many different construction methods and materials. Most walls, however, do have some common design aspects. These aspects include wall angles, faceted and nonfaceted climbing features, anchors, holds, surface texture, landing surface, space requirements, ventilation, access and egress, unsupervised use prevention, and structurally sound and appropriate design.

Wall Angles

The angle or angles of a wall, the number of faceted (smaller angled faces) features a wall has, and the number and variety of climbing features built into a wall are very important design considerations. Plain vertical walls with no faceted faces and limited climbing features may be appropriate for certain groups of participants (or your budget), but these walls lack the variety necessary to meet the needs of a diverse clientele with different interests, abilities, and goals. The more features your wall has, the greater the possible options for teaching, for varied climbing movements, for physical training, and for preventing burnout from lack of interest. Match the wall to its potential uses, but don't pay for items that will not be used once in operation.

Slabs

Wall angles may be slab (less than vertical), vertical, or overhanging. Vertical and overhanging angles are used most commonly in climbing wall designs. Slabs have limited usefulness for most climbing walls, particularly tall walls. They are the easiest physically to climb and are sometimes incorporated into bouldering walls and some tall walls for elementary age children, beginners, or climbers with little upper body strength. Most climbing wall manufacturers today do not recommend slabs as a worthwhile aspect of a climbing wall. People starting out on easy slabs soon want to move on. Slabs also do not offer much potential for physical training benefits or the variety necessary to hold climber interest. When slabs are incorporated into a tall wall design, it is usually as a small aspect of a larger wall featuring vertical or overhanging angles. Slabs are good for teaching correct body position and movement for low-angle climbing. However, falls on slabs have a higher potential for causing abrasion injuries because of possible sliding of the climber's body down the slab surface and the attached holds. Properly designed slabs on a bouldering or tall wall should extend all the way to the top of the wall or as high as climbing is allowed above the start of the slab feature.

Vertical or overhanging climbing routes should not be built above slab features on a wall. To do so creates a potential impact hazard for climbers if they were to fall from the vertical or overhanging section above onto the slab that sticks out below.

Vertical

A vertical wall angle (straight up at a 90-degree angle) is the place to start for most climbing walls, especially for walls to be used by older children and adults. Vertical walls provide a bigger variety of climbing possibilities and challenges than slabs do. They are very suitable for older beginners and intermediates, but they can provide some climbing and physical training benefits for advanced climbers as well when good route setting and hold selection are implemented. The drawback to pure vertical walls is that they limit some climbing possibilities, particularly in the potential benefits of physical training, as compared to outward leaning walls or vertical walls with overhanging features.

Overhanging

Wall angles that lean outward somewhat from the 90-degree vertical angle (less than a 90-degree angle) can increase the difficulty, climbing variety, and physical training potential of a wall. Overhanging walls also tend to hold the interest of climbers longer. Beginners who have limited upper body strength may not be best served by starting out on overhanging walls, especially greatly overhanging walls. However, overhanging walls suit advanced climbers' needs very well, especially if coupled with strategically placed ceilings of varying degrees of difficulty. Overhanging wall routes can be made more user friendly to climbers with less upper body strength by using large, easy-to-grip holds for hands and feet.

Faceted Climbing Features

Besides slabs, vertical sections, and sections of wall that are overhanging, there are many other types of short angles that can be built into a wall. These other angles create a multitude of smaller angled faces (facets). Where two facets come together you can get a variety of climbing features such as arêtes, inside corners and dihedrals, outside corners, ceilings of various angles, mantle shelves, buttresses, and chimneys (figure 2.9). Better walls have a variety of built-in facets of varying angles, and the features created when two or more facets join together are readily available in climbing walls made from a variety of construction methods, from plywood-surfaced climbing walls to walls made with materials that can be sculpted. Flat walls cost less to construct but are less visibly aesthetic, less interesting to climb on, and offer fewer climbing technique options.

Although faceted features add variety and climbing techniques to a wall, they also add to potential geometric hazards and safety concerns that should be addressed, ideally in the design stage.

FIGURE 2.9   Facets.
© Nicros

GEOMETRIC HAZARDS AND SAFETY CONSIDERATIONS

Geometric hazards may be any features that a falling, swinging, or ascending climber might strike or be injured by; or they may be features that create potentially hazardous drops or excessive swings if a climber falls off of them. Geometric hazards often occur wherever varying wall angles or faceted angles come together and wherever wall features project out or in from the wall surface.

Ceilings, for example, create many design challenges to mitigate potential geometric hazards they may pose if poorly designed. Ceilings are horizontal roofs that extend out varying distances from the primary wall surface (figure 2.10). They are a challenging climbing feature when incorporated into a vertical or overhanging wall. You should not see a ceiling (or a vertical wall for that matter) located above a slab, since that would create a potentially hazardous situation where a climber falling from the ceiling could fall onto the slab surface and injure his body, or worse, his head. Ceilings can be small and easy to pass, with big holds or

(continued)

FIGURE 2.10   Ceiling.
© Nicros

a design that allows climbers to reach over to holds on the vertical wall above; they can also be very strenuous and difficult with small holds and long horizontal aspects requiring the climber to lie out horizontally to move under the roof. You should give attention to the size, placement, and height above the landing surface of ceilings on any bouldering or tall wall.

Ceilings on bouldering walls, particularly large ones, should not be too high—approximately eight feet (2.5 meters)—and they require well-trained spotters who are physically capable of preventing a falling boulderer from landing on her butt, back, neck, or head. Deep bouldering ceilings that force the boulderer into a totally horizontal laid-out position are difficult to spot effectively. Bouldering ceilings should not be too low, forcing spotters to have to bend over to properly position themselves, since spotting a falling boulderer may create undue stress on the spotter's back or other body parts.

On tall walls, ceilings need to be situated high enough on the wall to provide adequate space to catch the falling climber with the belay rope. On a top-rope wall route, adequate backward swing and down-drop space should be provided. How much space is needed depends on roof depth (distance it extends out from the main wall) and how close the ceiling is to the landing surface. An incorrectly designed ceiling—too close to the floor (too deep for the distance it is from the floor)—has the potential to allow a climber falling from under the ceiling of the overhang to strike the floor on the down-drop and backswing of a top-rope belay. The deeper the horizontal aspect of the ceiling, the more clear space behind the climb is required to accommodate for backswing on top-roped walls.

Lead climbing a ceiling route does not require as much backswing space from the wall because the falling climber tends to fall either down or down and swinging back toward the wall under the ceiling, which can be a hazard to the climber if the protection anchors are not properly placed in the ceiling roof to prevent a forceful drop and swing into the vertical wall section below. Helmets are definitely more called for in lead climbing, particularly with ceilings.

As stated previously, you must consider the hazards to a falling or ascending climber that faceted and other wall features may present if poorly designed, improperly located, or belayed incorrectly. Professional consultation is very valuable when designing climbing walls that minimize geometric hazards while incorporating a variety of faceted and nonfaceted climbing features. You should note that good climbing wall designs can reduce but not totally eliminate geometric hazards. The following list identifies some geometric hazard and safety considerations, but in no way should it be construed that those listed are the only considerations that need to be addressed. You should seek out design advice from professional climbing wall designers and engineers, particularly ones who have had previous experience designing walls similar to the wall you are planning.

Examples of Geometric Safety Considerations

- Can an unanchored belayer be pulled up into a low ceiling on the wall when stopping the fall of a much heavier climber, especially in a lead-climbing situation?

- Can a falling climber drop onto some feature, such as a ledge, mantle shelf, or slab, when climbing vertical or overhanging routes above such features?

- Will a falling climber pendulum into a feature, such as an inside corner side wall or a feature projecting out from the wall surface significantly, if she is climbing out to the side of the top running anchor in top-roping or the last protection anchor she has clipped to in lead climbing?

- If a climber falls while climbing a feature such as an arête or outside corner, can that feature injure her if she slides down it during the fall?

- Can a climber get his feet, hands, or fingers stuck in a hold or feature that would cause injury to the climber by not releasing his hand or foot in a fall?

- Can a climber who attempts to top out (stand on top of the wall structure) be cut by sharp edges of the top of the wall? Will he be able to grab light fixtures? Can he hit his head on sharp objects situated above the top of the wall?

- Is a ceiling high enough off the landing surface, considering the horizontal depth of the ceiling from the main wall surface, so that if top-roping the route a climber falling from under the ceiling will not hit the landing surface as he drops and swings backward? And is there enough clear backswing space provided so the climber will not hit an object or wall behind him as he swings backward from the climbing wall?

- Are lead-climbing protection anchors properly positioned and spaced in relation to climbing wall features present? Are protection anchors under ceilings for lead climbing positioned properly on the ceiling to prevent a falling lead climber from swinging with force back into the vertical wall under the ceiling?

- Are the top-rope belay top running anchors positioned properly, directly above the top-rope climbing routes on the wall?

- Are all provided floor anchors recessed into the floor to prevent people on the landing surface from tripping over them when not in use?

Ideally, geometric hazards and safety concerns should be recognized and addressed during the design phase of planning a climbing wall. You must remember, though, that even the most thoroughly designed wall may have geometric hazards present themselves once the wall is constructed and in operation. These hazards need to be addressed as they appear. Documentation of near misses and accidents, and awareness of trends, should be ongoing for the life of the wall. Having a "what if" attitude is also useful. If a climber did something, what would be the consequences of a fall? If hazardous, you then address that behavior or aspect to mitigate the potential geometric hazards you identified. For example, you might change a route's holds or location, instruct climbers about the hazards and restrict them from doing certain behaviors, require all lead climbers to clip all protection anchors on a lead-climbing route, require climbers to wear helmets, and so on. Again, try to address geometric hazards and safety concerns during the design phase, but keep an open eye and awareness for ones you missed that show themselves during operation.

Nonfaceted Climbing Features

Climbing walls often have many climbing features that are not created by joining facets. These include features such as pockets, flakes, grooves, horizontal cracks, vertical cracks for jamming, bulges, and so on (figure 2.11).

Commercially built walls made with special sculptured exterior surfaces offer the potential for a greater variety of features and more natural, rocklike quality. Pockets, flakes, grooves, and cracks can be sculpted directly into the surface coating, as can fingerholds and footholds. Bulges can also be put onto the wall. In homemade and commercially built walls with plywood as the exterior surface, it is more difficult to add some of these features, but it is possible to put in vertical finger, hand, and foot jam cracks. Finger, hand, and foot jam cracks made of wood are not as aesthetically pleasing as the real thing, but they work fairly well. Splinters, as well as sharp edges, are a potential problem if cracks made of wood are designed poorly. Beware of making vertical finger-jamming cracks that constrict to less than finger size lower down in the crack. Climbers who are finger jamming up the crack, and then fall, may accidentally wedge their fingers in the lower constriction if they do not get their fingers out of the crack during the fall.

FIGURE 2.11 Pockets, flakes, and grooves.
© Nicros

Anchors

The type, location, and use of anchors for a climbing wall are important design considerations. Even though anchors could be considered equipment, and the way they are used could be considered technique, the equipment you will use and the techniques they may require need to be understood when designing a climbing wall. Therefore, a detailed look at anchors and their use is provided here, rather than in later chapters.

Three types of anchors are commonly used with tall climbing walls: top-rope running anchors, lead-climbing protection anchors, and floor anchors. All types of climbing wall anchors are critical parts of a climbing wall system and must not fail. Designing and constructing your own anchors is ill-advised. Using the services of professional designers and installers is very important from a hazard and liability standpoint. It is recommended that all climbing wall anchors meet CWIG design standards. Contact the CWA (see appendix B) for more information on these highly technical standards. The CWIG standards for anchors are based on worst cases loading on the top piece of protection in the system during a fall. Currently, all anchors must be able to sustain an impact force of 20 kilonewtons (or 4400 foot-pounds). CWIG worst-case impact force is calculated using UIAA-approved dynamic climbing rope. If ropes of less dynamic quality (such as static line) are used for belaying purposes, the maximum worst-case impact forces may be higher than CWIG standards, necessitating stronger anchors and wall support structures.

Top-Rope Running Anchors

For top-rope belaying, the belay rope runs from the climber's harness, up over or through an upper running anchor, and back down to the belayer on the floor behind the route being climbed. A number of appropriate top-rope running anchors exist. Two common top-rope running anchors are ones using large-diameter round steel bars secured to the wall support structure above the route, and ones using two protection anchor bolts, or other fixtures, to which either quickdraws or appropriate-sized chains are attached (figure 2.12). Locking steel carabiners or one-half-inch steel rapid links are used to secure the draws or chains to the anchors, and to secure the belay rope to the outer ends of the draws or chains. If the two protection anchors are placed side by side, make sure the angle of the draws or chains after being secured to the belay rope is less than 90 degrees. This prevents a severe multiplication of force from being placed on each anchor during a fall. The lesser the angle, the smaller the impact force exerted on each of the supporting anchors. Both anchors and draws or chains should be equally weighted as well when any force is put on the top-rope upper anchor, such as occurs when a fall is caught. The belay rope goes over the bar or through both carabiners or both rapid links of the double protection anchor/bolt system. The top-rope upper anchors

FIGURE 2.12   Top-roping anchors.

should be situated directly over the climb to be belayed in order to prevent pendulum swings by falling climbers. They must be strong enough to hold any potential belayed fall possible on the wall, and they are usually secured directly to the support structure of the wall itself.

Lead-Climbing Protection Anchors

Lead-climbing protection anchors are special climbing protection bolts with hangers to which quickdraws are attached. The quickdraw will be attached to the bolt hanger with either a one-half-inch rapid link (most common and cost-effective method) or a locking carabiner, and it will have a carabiner on the outer end to which the lead climber clips his belay rope in a running fashion. The belay rope then continues back down to the belayer on the floor. As the climber ascends, he will clip into each protection bolt on the route as he comes to them. Most climbing wall programs that are set up for lead climbing will preattach the quickdraws on the routes rather than have climbers place them as they climb. This allows for a greater safety margin in the lead-climbing system by helping to prevent improper attachment of carabiners to bolt hangers. The practice of using locking carabiners or rapid links, with the gates screwing downward to lock them to the hangers, also creates a stronger system that helps to prevent accidental detachments of the draw from the hanger during a fall. Some climbing wall operations also use a locking carabiner on the outer portion of the first bolt or quickdraw on the route. This helps minimize the possibility of the belay rope unclipping from the carabiner due to an upward pull on the first attachment point after the climber has clipped to subsequent anchors above and the belayer is not directly under the first anchor clipped.

Lead-climbing routes also need to have a top-rope double bolt and chain anchor system at the top of the route, with locking carabiners at the end of both chains so that the lead climber can clip through both carabiners with the belay rope, lock the gate of both carabiners, and then be properly lowered to the ground by the belayer. This same double anchor can be designed to be used as a top-rope running anchor as well, though some walls use separate systems for the same route. Steel locking carabiners are better for this purpose since they are far more durable and therefore more cost effective than aluminum carabiners. Aluminum carabiners are generally used for the protection anchor quickdraws since they are less expensive. Oval and pear-shaped locking carabiners have a slight advantage in terms of functional use when being secured to the outer ends of draws or chains being used as top-rope running anchors or to lower lead climbers at the top of climbs. Ideally, the two locking carabiners on the ends of double top-rope running anchors should be attached to the draws or chains in a manner that reverses and opposes the gates of the two carabiners after the belay rope is attached to them in a running manner. This helps to prevent accidental detachment of the belay rope if the gates of the carabiners open accidentally. The gates should also be attached so they screw down with gravity rather than upward.

Floor Anchors

Floor anchors located properly at the bottom of each climbing route on a tall wall are used to secure a belayer down when he catches a belayed fall (figure 2.13). It is common practice to belay unanchored at most climbing walls since belays should be as dynamic as possible without compromising the climber's comfort and welfare. A dynamic belay lowers the maximum impact forces on the wall support structure and the climber's body when stopping a falling climber with the belay rope. There are times, however, when a belayer might need to be secured to prevent him from being lifted completely off the floor or pulled forward significantly while catching a fall. A belayer who weighs significantly less than the climber should be secured down in some manner so he does not get pulled off the floor or yanked along the floor. This is particularly true for lead climb belaying where impact forces of a fall tend to be higher. Securing beginning belayers is also worthwhile, as is securing belayers who are under ceilings located relatively close to the floor. Floor anchors, where provided, should be located under the route's top-rope running anchor or lead-climbing protection anchors. The floor anchors should only be as far back from the climbing route as necessary to be out of the fall or landing zone of the climb and where the belayer cannot be hit by

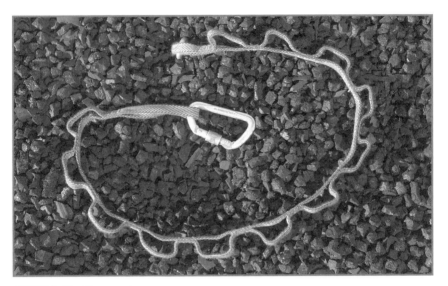

FIGURE 2.13 Floor anchors.

the backswing of a climber falling low on the route. This is especially important in lead-climbing situations where having floor anchors far away from the route makes for sharp rope angles and upward pull on the first protection anchor of the route. Floor anchors may or may not be recessed into the floor. Recessed anchors help prevent people from accidentally tripping over them, but they must be inspected often for proper working ability, since they are not visible (particularly floor anchors hidden under loose floor surface materials).

A belayer uses a floor anchor by attaching a sling or daisy chain, which is secured to the anchor, to the bottom of his harness belay loop with a locking carabiner (figure 2.14). The sling should be just long enough to allow the belayer to stand upright next to the anchor. Long, loose anchor slings are not good because they allow a belayer to be jerked upward or forward when stopping a fall, and this multiplies the impact forces on the floor anchor. An alternative method of securing the belayer to the anchor is to have the belayer tie into the end of the belay rope that is not attached to the climber, and then take this rope (running from the belayer's harness) and secure it to a locking carabiner attached to the floor anchor with a figure eight loop. Once the belayer is anchored in, he uses a locking carabiner to attach a belay device to the upper part of his harness belay loop (when anchored in with a sling) or to the upper part of his harness belay loop *and* to the figure eight loop secured to his harness (when anchoring in with the belay rope). The belayer then secures the belay rope to the belay device. It is recommended that the belayer have the belay device secured to his harness belay loop while belaying. Belayers should not belay directly off an anchor only, since in the event of floor anchor failure, the belayer could not stop a fall.

Alternative methods of anchoring a belayer can be used when necessary in situations where floor anchors have not been installed. Some gyms use a five-gallon (18-liter) bucket filled with hardened concrete into which a five-eighth-inch steel eyebolt has been secured. The bucket is moved to the proper location under the route to be climbed, and the belayer anchors into the eyebolt appropriately and belays off his harness belay loop. Another portable method has the belayer anchoring into a rubberized weightlifting plate of appropriate weight. A sling is girth-hitched around the weight by putting it through the eye of the plate and is then attached to the belayer's harness belay loop.

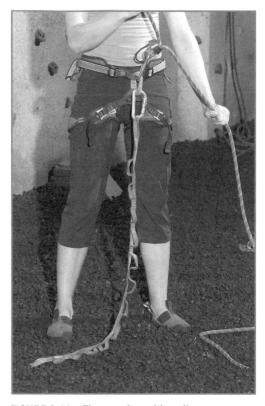

FIGURE 2.14   Floor anchor with a sling.

One last portable anchoring system uses another person as the anchor weight. A short sling runs from the belay loop of the anchorperson's harness to the harness belay loop of the belayer, who then belays off his harness belay loop as usual. The belay anchorperson stands immediately behind the belayer.

Holds

Climbing holds are what climbers use with their hands and feet to ascend a climbing wall. Holds are attached to the wall in some manner or are sculpted into the surface material of the wall before it hardens. Holds that are attached to the wall generally employ T-nut inserts or other similar threaded devices that are secured to the plywood or alternative wall surface. Screw-on holds are then attached to these devices. These systems allow for holds to be changed. Some simple, homebuilt walls may use holds that are glued onto the wall with adhesives. There are many different types of adhesives, so be sure you use the right adhesive for your materials by consulting an expert on adhesives. Also be aware that glue-on holds have a bad habit of popping off under average use no matter how good the adhesive used is. Screw-on or bolt-on holds allow for variety on a wall. Glue-on holds do not. Typically, for climbing walls employing screw-on holds, a high number of T-nut or similar device inserts are placed into the entire climbing surface, usually in a random pattern rather than a grid pattern. This allows individual holds or entire routes to be changed by replacing holds or moving holds to new locations on the wall. You can simply replace one hold with a hold of a different shape or degree of difficulty.

Sculpted holds provide a more realistic rock-climbing experience, but they can't be changed. Most sculpted walls incorporate a plethora of screw-on holds as well so that routes and difficulty levels can be changed to meet and maintain climber interest, to enhance training possibilities, and to simulate a greater variety of movements required on real rock and climbing techniques.

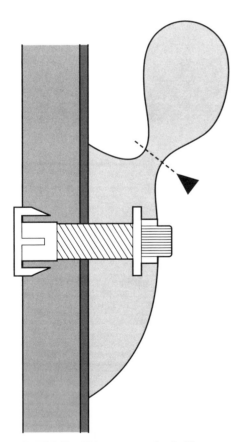

FIGURE 2.15 Thin cross-section hold.

Hold Materials

Attachable holds can be made of a number of materials. These include plastics, wood, ceramics, and rock. Each has its own benefits and drawbacks, but plastic holds are most often used on climbing walls.

Plastic Holds Holds made of plastic are by far the most popular type of screw-on and bolt-on holds in use on climbing walls. Plastic holds can be manufactured in a great variety of shapes, sizes, and colors. They are usually made of some type of polyester resin or polyurethane material. Polyester holds offer better texture and rocklike feel, and they are stronger but more brittle than polyurethane holds. Polyurethane-based holds tend to be more flexible and durable than polyester-resin-based holds, but they also tend to feel more plastic than rocklike. Polyurethane holds are often preferred on walls or specific locations on walls with uneven surfaces. Ideally, however, all types of plastic holds should be placed on flat wall surfaces to help prevent breakage. You should try out a variety of available holds from the numerous manufacturers to find the styles and the feel you prefer for your wall before buying.

Plastic holds need to be well designed to help prevent breakage. Holds with very thin cross sections in an unsupported part of the hold may break easily if loaded (pulled or pushed on) from certain directions (figure 2.15). Holds may also break due to improper setting such as on an uneven wall surface, overtightening of the attachment bolts, excessive use or force, ultraviolet degradation (outdoors especially), and from being dropped from a height and then placed back on a wall.

Wooden Holds   Definitely old school, wooden block holds provide a cheap alternative, but if at all possible you should go with synthetic holds because of their texture and more realistic feel and use. Wooden blocks do not offer the variety plastic holds do, and they are more prone to breaking due to hidden flaws (weaknesses) in the wood itself. Wooden blocks are shaped and beveled in varying widths and sizes. They can be attached to a wall's surface using T-nuts and inserts (or similar methods), lag screwed, or glued directly onto the wall. Use a hard wood or semihard wood that does not check. Mahogany works well. Poplar is okay; pine and oak are not as acceptable. A good resource for building and using wooden block holds is Karl Rohnke's book, *High Profile* (see appendix B).

Rock Holds   Rock holds feel realistic and are less expensive than plastic holds, but rock is not a common hold material on most climbing walls today. Rock holds tend to be heavy, may have hidden weaknesses that you cannot see (which make them more prone to breakage), and are difficult to use with T-nut or other insert attachment methods. They are more commonly used on homemade walls and preexisting concrete walls where they are glued on with an appropriate adhesive. If you plan to glue on rock holds, consult an expert on what adhesive to use for your type of rock and wall surface to get the best attachment. Remember, though, that glued-on holds often come unglued after a little use. Glued-on holds limit the variety of options on a wall since it is difficult to move them.

Selecting Holds

Holds come in a variety of shapes and sizes to match almost any climbing situation. The array of holds being churned out by more than 20 climbing wall companies can be dazzling (e.g., jibs, alien babies, supercakes, chubs, and footsies), requiring a multitude of moves (e.g., dynos, gorilla cranks, tricky bits, and Frankenstein lie-backs). One climbing wall company, Nicros, offers over 1000 different handhold shapes. There are so many holds on the market that it is difficult to describe a typical hold. However, manufacturers regularly refer to several different types of holds described as roofs, slopers, edges, crimps, pinches, and pockets. The following are examples of common types of holds:

- **Roofs (sometimes referred to as jugs or roof holds) and buckets.** Big or rounded holds where fingers can conform to the natural curvature of the hold (open grip). Intuitively, the open grip is least stressful on both joints and tendons. These tendon-friendly and enjoyable holds should be used whenever possible, whether learning to climb, warming up, or working on endurance. Roofs with a gripping surface that tilts in toward the wall provide the best holds.

- **Slopers.** Rounded holds that are smaller than jugs and where the gripping surface is difficult because it slopes down and away from the wall. Regardless of the size of a hold, it is the edge that places the greatest amount of pressure on your fingers or hand. Slopers (and also edges, crimps, pinches, and pockets) are tendon loading—good for training to increase tendon strength if you do so wisely.

- **Edges.** Flat-topped holds reminiscent of small shelves just big enough to be held with the first digit or two of all four fingers (cling grip, which is more stressful on tendons and fingers, thus prudent use should be considered).

- **Crimps.** Flat holds that are smaller than edges. These small holds permit using only the first digit of the finger (vertical grip, also stressful on tendons and fingers).

- **Pinches.** Small knobs to be grasped with the thumb and a finger, usually the side of the index finger (pinch grip). These holds can be very difficult depending on the size and angle of the wall. They tend to be some of the best holds for training purposes because they require grasping, pulling, and clasping as well as require more concentration.

- **Pockets.** Holds with holes into which one or more fingers may be inserted (pocket grip), sometimes requiring stacking the fingers on top of each other for increased torque. Using a single digit places considerable strain on individual tendons and may cause injury. Avoid setting these where one pocket is used to pull substantial weight.

Size and Shape of Holds

Selecting a variety of hold sizes and shapes to provide climbing experiences and training that are appropriate for a range of abilities, training interests, styles, and climber safety is very important in the design of a good climbing wall. Holds come in small, medium, and large sizes. They also come in a variety of shapes such as crimps, pockets, buckets, knobs, slopers, underclings, pinches, and so on (figure 2.16). Hold size and shape affect how easy or difficult a hold is to grip with the hands and feet.

FIGURE 2.16   Holds come in a variety of shapes and sizes.
© Gopher Sport

Small Holds   Small holds are usually designed for working on footwork or as difficult handholds to increase the difficulty of a route and work on finger strength. Smaller holds tend to be used on vertical and slab angled wall sections. The excessive use of difficult small handholds can potentially lead to increased finger and elbow tendon or ligament injuries. Monodigit pockets, which are small holds where only one digit can be used in a small hole in the hold, are often cited for causing finger tendon injuries. Monodigit pockets should not be placed where they are the handhold for difficult crux moves on climbing routes. To do so invites finger injuries.

Medium Holds   Medium-sized holds tend to be the workhorse of holds used on a wall. They commonly represent approximately one-third of the total holds on a wall, with a higher percentage being found on walls serving primarily better climbers. Medium-sized holds help to prevent overcrimping by allowing the climber to grip the hold with all her fingers well supported on the hold up to at least the middle finger joints. This helps relieve some of the stress on the fingers and arms, such as occurs when only the fingertips can be used on small holds. Medium holds can be designed to be easy or difficult to grip when climbing.

Large Holds   Large holds represent approximately one-third of the total holds on the average climbing wall. They are used on a route to make the route easier and are scattered around on less steep terrain to provide resting spots for hands and feet. Large, easy-to-grip holds are also often put onto overhanging wall surfaces and ceilings to provide positive holds on steep terrain, which, while giving a good "pump," lessens the risk of finger and elbow soft tissue injury from overexertion or repetitive use. This concept also applies to providing large holds on vertical terrain for beginners who have weaker hand and upper body strength and less endurance.

You should consult with experienced climbing hold manufacturers and route setters during the wall design phase to determine a good mix of holds to purchase for your wall. (Refer to appendix B for resources.)

Experienced climbing wall route setters use a variety of hold sizes and shapes, coupled with the wall angles and features, and the location of holds, to create routes on a wall of varying difficulties. Easy routes on vertical walls are composed primarily of medium size holds with some large holds and some small foot-designated holds. Difficult routes on vertical walls will have a larger sampling of small fingerholds and footholds, with fewer large, easy holds, and a lesser number of medium holds mixed in. Strong climbers can grip smaller holds on steeper walls, while weaker and less experienced climbers require easier, larger holds to make progress. Overhanging routes need larger holds to allow progress and lessen the likelihood of finger and elbow injuries.

Lead-climbing routes require positive resting spots at each protection anchor so the lead climber can clip into the anchor without a high risk of falling as she tries to clip her belay rope into the protection anchor quickdraw. The more difficult moves on a lead climb should be on holds placed a short distance above each anchor, with easy moves set from the floor up to the first protection anchor. The more difficult moves on a tall climbing wall should be set in the middle to upper portions of the wall. Difficult moves close to the floor on tall walls are less desirable since it is more difficult for a belayer to prevent a falling climber from contacting the ground (due to less time to react and the initial stretch of the belay rope when stopping a fall). Bouldering walls should have the more difficult moves set closer to the landing surface to reduce the chance of injury in a fall and to make it easier to spot a falling boulderer.

Quantity of Holds

Besides deciding what types of holds to buy and how they will be attached to the wall, you should also determine how many holds you will need to provide a good experience. A commonly quoted figure is .31 handholds per square foot, or said another way, 10 handholds for each 8-by-4-foot (2.5-by-1.2-meter)—32 square feet (2.9 square meters)—sheet of plywood.

Bouldering walls often use a higher number of holds per square foot as compared to tall walls.

A few final comments on holds. First, the overall shape of a hold is as important as the feel or texture. A well-designed hold distributes pressure across the fingers and is therefore tendon friendly. Manufacturers today take safety into consideration in their craftsmanship—a welcome change from the tendon-tearing holds of just a few years ago. Nevertheless, when selecting holds, you should choose imaginative shapes devoid of sharp edges or corners. Look for designs that have either flat surfaces that end with rounded edges or gradually convex or concave bulges that fit the natural form of the hand. If a hold is uncomfortable in certain placements, simply rotating it may improve climbers' comfort and safety. Second, since repetition is a main cause of injury, use a variety of holds that will train muscles and tendons more completely. Variety also keeps routes interesting. Third, the strength of a hold is an additional consideration. Holds that break can also cause injuries.

We recommend that holds be purchased only from companies that show evidence of a responsible vendor attitude; that is, those who carry product liability insurance and who properly design or engineer their products to include testing their holds according to industry standards. For more information on resources, refer to appendix B.

Surface Texture

Climbing walls are best finished with textured surfaces that are durable, provide friction for footwork moves, and help protect the underlying wall construction materials. It is also nice if the surface texture simulates the look, feel, and aesthetics of real rock. Homebuilt walls made with plywood sheets can be used without surface coverings, but they are generally thought to be better with some covering. Plywood may be painted with durable acrylic (water-based) paints or alkyd (oil-based) paints. Acrylic paints today are durable, offer easy cleanup, and are less toxic to the environment. Special climbing wall pretexturized paints are available from some wall manufacturers; when used according to the manufacturer's application directions, these paints offer excellent results. Commercially constructed walls using plywood sheeting may be painted with textured paints; or they may be coated with a thin or thick layer of rocklike material made of special cements or fiberglass with a resinous concrete coating, which then may be sculpted when wet to provide rocklike features and holds on the surface itself. Plywood walls painted with texturized paint are less expensive and require either glue-on holds or the more common screw-on insert type holds. Coated plywood walls give a more realistic rocklike surface and can be made to feel much like real rock, with holds and cracks like a real rock. They may include a combination of surface holds and screw-on holds to add greater variety. The more sculpting that takes place, the greater the cost of the wall in general, as compared to a flat textured surface.

Landing Surface

The purpose of a good landing surface is to provide lower-impact landings for the feet and body of a climber when jumping, falling, or being lowered onto the landing surface. All climbing walls, whether bouldering or tall walls, should have a durable landing surface of appropriate density to lessen the impact of falls or landings onto the landing surface—underneath all climbing and lowering aspects of the wall. The landing surface or fall zone should be free of gaps in the surface that someone could step through. It should also be spaced an adequate distance out behind and to each side of the climbing surfaces to help prevent potential impacts with hard surfaces, accounting for maximum swing radiuses and for climbers pushing off the wall during falls or while being lowered. Landing surfaces should be free of any equipment or objects that the falling or lowering climber could come in contact with. Belayers should also not have anything underfoot or surrounding them that they might accidentally step onto or be pulled into along the floor. Adequate landing surface depth and material density are dictated by maximum fall height, particularly for bouldering walls.

Bouldering walls, in particular, need landing surfaces that adequately lessen the impact from falls and jumping down from heights onto the landing surface. Often, additional pads are used under boulderers to help cushion landings, but pads placed on top of the regular landing surface can be an extra hazard to the boulderer if misplaced, which frequently happens. A common bouldering injury occurs when landing on the edge of the pad, or a gap between two pads, and rolling an ankle, causing a sprain or break. Boulderers should be educated on how to use additional pads correctly before being allowed to use them. Even better is to have a uniform, gapless landing surface over the entire climbing wall area that is suitable for bouldering without the need for additional pads.

There are many types of materials that can be used as appropriate landing surfaces under climbing walls. For outdoor walls, materials associated with playgrounds are often used, including shredded bark mulch, wood chips, fine sand, and pea gravel of appropriate size. Pea gravel and sand are less desirable since they create accelerated wear on belay ropes and climbing hardware by being gritty and dusty. Climbers also do not like having sand and the rock dust of pea gravel sticking onto their shoes when starting to climb. It makes for less secure footing during climbs. For indoor climbing walls, natural materials are usually avoided for landing surfaces (if money is not a concern) since these materials tend to create a dusty atmosphere that is wearing on equipment and hard on the lungs, and the dust or material can be tracked around into other building areas, adding to cleanup costs. Most climbers dislike sand as well because it sticks to their climbing shoes somewhat, dirties the shoe rubber, and interferes with good footwork if they don't rub it off before climbing.

Gymnastics style landing mats are used for many less elaborate walls (the mats are often covered with a more durable full-coverage surface such as a carpet). Gymnastics mats should be secured together in an acceptable manner to prevent gaps between adjacent mats; this will prevent injuries from stepping or landing in gaps between adjacent mats. Many climbing wall construction companies can provide specialty landing surfaces that may add to the expense but are usually more durable and aesthetically pleasing. Cleanup operations are often simpler as well. Some companies utilize carpet and foam systems. One company offers a rubber and foam landing surface that is poured in place, which eliminates seams, and that is covered with a choice of two different durable rubber top surfaces. These surfaces can also be used outdoors with special materials added. Some manufacturers offer less expensive, but highly functional, landing surfaces made from a blend of shredded tire rubber and other rubber materials. These surfaces are durable and tend to create less dust than natural materials. They are often touted as being the best low-cost landing surface alternative. When considering shredded rubber landing surfaces, you should be sure not to purchase ones that have been made with any shredded tire rubber containing steel-belted ribbons.

Space Requirements

Space requirements fall into a number of categories, including how much space is required surrounding the climbing, belaying, and spotting area; space requirements for the active climbing, belaying, and spotting floor area; how much space to allow between routes on the wall; head space at the top of the climbing routes; side clearance considerations; and the need for space behind the wall surface structure.

Surrounding Room Space

An important climbing wall design consideration is planning adequate space surrounding the active climbing areas to allow movement of people not involved in the actual climbing process. You may want to delineate these areas so they are clearly recognizable. It is best not to allow people to move through active climbing areas underneath the climbs or between belayers or spotters and the routes being climbed. This concept is coupled in many ways with facility design considerations related to traffic flow control. Also, if you want to allow spectators in your climbing facility, space should be planned for them.

Active Floor Area

The active floor area includes all climbing, belaying, and spotting activities that are actively occurring in your facility, and all landing surfaces. This area should include enough space to accommodate any backswings and side swings from climbing routes that may happen to belayed climbers and should extend out to the wall's side edges. Active floor space must be designed to be large enough to accommodate the number of climbers and belayers or spotters you plan to have active at one time so that they are not jammed together and will not interfere with each other.

Space Between Climbers and Routes

Consideration should be given to how far apart active climbing routes on a wall need to be. This affects how wide the climbing surface area will need to be, taking into account the number of active climbing routes you wish to have going on at one time. You do not want adjacent climbers obstructing each other, competing for holds, stepping on each others' hands, or falling onto or swinging into (pendulum) each other if a fall occurs. A pendulum fall can occur any time a belayed climber moves out to either side of a route's vertical line running from the floor to where the belay rope goes through or around the highest running anchor point. There is no magic number for how far apart adjacent climbers need to be. The level of direct supervision of climbing activities greatly affects spacing between climbers. Thoughtful, closely supervised climbing activities allow for less spacing between climbers, with four feet (121 centimeters) between climbers being a common minimum spacing, particularly with portable climbing walls. On walls operating with minimal direct supervision, greater spacing between adjacent climbers is necessary. In large gyms and on large walls where minimal direct supervision is provided, a width of six to eight feet (182 to 243 centimeters) between climbers can be more secure and more comfortable for the climbers.

Headroom

Unobstructed headroom is required from any structural items in the ceiling above the wall, such as beams, joists, and so forth; from any mechanical objects including wiring, light fixtures, and air ducts; and from sharp corners and edges. There should not be anything hazardous to a climber's touch within the reach of a climber who is at the top or side of a wall.

Side Clearance

Climbing walls, except those that provide for climbing all the way around the structure, should have distinct terminal side edges. There should be no structural or mechanical aspects at the edges that a climber can grab onto or come in contact with. It is recommended that a blank space without holds or inserts for holds be located in from the side edges of the wall.

The first holds and climbing routes should start far enough in from the sides of the wall to prevent a climber from being able to grab or contact the edge of the wall either by swinging like a pendulum or by reaching.

Space Behind the Wall

Some methods of constructing a climbing wall require considerable space behind the wall's climbing surface and the supporting structure. This is particularly true of tall walls. If a wall is to be constructed inside a preexisting room or facility, the thickness of the wall and back-space requirements, as well as the space requirements in front of the wall, should be taken into account during the design phase. Certain designs may not be suitable for a specified location, or another location may need to be considered if desired design features require larger space.

Ventilation

Providing adequate ventilation systems will enhance the climbing experience of wall users and will help to suppress dust levels. Excessive dust on belay ropes and other equipment accelerates wear on equipment. Poorly ventilated climbing walls, particularly in cramped spaces, can quickly take on the qualities of a poorly ventilated wrestling or locker room.

Access and Egress Locations

How people will enter and exit the climbing wall facility is an important design consideration. Access and egress points should be located strategically. They should prevent uncontrolled and unseen entry, should take into account emergency access and egress needs, and should prevent those who are entering and exiting the facility from interfering with climbing wall activity. Usually only one nonemergency entry/exit point is provided for participant use. A control point is usually set up at the entry/exit location, and all waivers are collected at this control location before participants enter the facility proper. Unauthorized or unsupervised use of climbing walls should be restricted.

Restricting Unsupervised Use

Most climbing walls are secured in some manner to try to prevent unauthorized use during nonsupervised times. How to do so needs to be considered during the design phase of the facility. It is much easier to design in methods of limiting access to a climbing wall than it is to try to add them after the wall has been built with no consideration given to limiting access. You need to be aware that unlimited use climbing walls can be considered in many legal jurisdictions to be an "attractive nuisance." There are, however, a few examples of unsupervised outdoor bouldering walls, which are usually lumped under the playground apparatus category. Restricting unauthorized and unsupervised use may be as simple as designing the climbing facility with lockable doors, but that is not always feasible, such as in multiuse recreation centers and schools. Some programs remove all the lower holds on their wall—usually up to 10 to 15 feet (3.0 to 4.5 meters) high—though this is time consuming, increases wear on the bolts securing holds to the wall, and increases the likelihood of breaking holds due to overtightening. In school gymnasiums with bouldering walls attached to the main gymnasium wall, some schools secure mats to the lower portions of the climbing surface to cover the holds (figure 2.17). Some climbing walls that are recessed into the wall of a larger multiuse open space have secure screens that can be pulled across the entrance to the climbing wall surface, similar to what you often see at closing time in malls.

Structurally Sound Design

It goes without saying that a climbing wall design must be structurally appropriate. A freestanding climbing wall may need to be structurally self-supporting and capable of supporting the stress of climbing activity, as well as other potential stresses such as seismic loads, hurricane loads, snow loads, and so on, which could affect the structure. Climbing walls

FIGURE 2.17 **Restricting unsupervised use.**

that will be attached to preexisting walls require that the preexisting wall be able to handle the extra load of the climbing wall structure and climbing activity. Existing floors and ceilings must also be able to support the stresses and weight of attached climbing wall structures. It is very important that licensed professional structural engineers, who are knowledgeable in climbing wall technology and construction, be consulted and used to approve final designs of climbing walls. This will help ensure that all applicable local, state, and federal codes are met and building permits are obtained; it will also ensure that applicable climbing wall industry standards, such as those of the CWIG or equivalent standards, are met when a climbing wall is designed and built.

Commercially built climbing walls are generally more aesthetically pleasing, durable, varied, more rocklike, and will hold the interest of repeat users better (figure 2.18). Commercial designers and manufacturers can build simple homebuilt style walls, but their forte is the design and construction of more realistic bouldering and tall wall structures, from small to very large and elaborate. Climbing wall designers and manufacturers can be with you at all stages of the wall planning and construction process, and they may even help in the operation phase of your wall by offering advice on effective methods to operate your wall. Their services should go beyond just building a wall for you. Using the services of a professional climbing wall designer or builder can also help programs in the area of risk management and liability. You need to be aware, though,

FIGURE 2.18   Well-designed wall.
© Nicros

that not all climbing wall designers and manufacturers are equal when it comes to quality, abilities, and services offered. Shop wisely.

Good commercial climbing wall manufacturers offer a variety of services designed to help you during some or all phases of design, construction, and operation. Some companies offer complete services, while others may specialize in one or more aspects (requiring the coordination of more than one company to complete the project). If you are planning to use more than one company, you should keep the number of companies used small to reduce potential incompatibility problems. Whether selecting one manufacturer for the entire process or a combination, the "team" should be able to design, engineer, and construct climbing walls that meet all applicable local, state, and federal codes for your location. Their construction methods should meet all climbing wall industry standards for your location, such as the CWIG standards. You should check the qualifications of the companies you employ. Ideally, they are active members of the CWA and other applicable professional organizations. They should also have practical experience with the design and construction of climbing walls similar to your project ideas.

Good commercial climbing wall manufacturers employ certified or licensed engineers, designers, and construction specialists. They are also insured for liability and will provide a warranty for their construction work once completed. They should be willing to supply a list of operating climbing walls they have built that are similar to the wall you have in mind so that you can visit the walls to see the quality of the work and contact the wall operators to determine their satisfaction. Most good companies also offer inspection services once your wall is in operation to help with risk management concerns and to attempt to keep your wall as free of hazards as possible (and keep the wall up-to-date regarding any changes in standards).

Once the wall is finished, the builder should be willing and able to assist you directly or by consultation with outfitting the facility, including equipment needs, staffing needs and training, operating procedures, route-setting information, maintenance, safety management concerns, and risk management procedures. The builder should be willing to assist you down the road if questions or problems arise.

Summary

The ultimate goal during the design phase of a climbing wall project is to take all the important design considerations relating to your project and situation and come up with a design brief that will guide the construction process. On small, simple projects, this might be done by the ultimate operator of the wall, but for large projects it is well worth using the services of qualified commercial climbing wall designers, engineers, and manufacturers. General items you might consider in developing a design brief include the following:

- Desired wall height
- Width of the wall
- Depth (thickness) of the wall, which is the distance that the top of the wall protrudes from the wall's base. Depth also includes any space needed behind the climbing wall surface to be able to inspect the support structure if necessary.
- Number of desired routes
- Who will be using the wall:
  - Beginners, intermediates, advanced climbers
  - Groups
  - Instructional use
  - Training
  - Participant age ranges
- Nature of the climbing (when designing a climbing wall, it is useful to specify how much of the wall will be devoted to each form of climbing):
  - Bouldering
  - Top-roping
  - Lead climbing
  - Rappelling
  - Competitions
- Wall features desired:
  - Wall angles
  - Faceted climbing features
  - Nonfaceted climbing features
  - Types of holds
- Wall construction method desired and type of surface
- Location of wall and structural or engineering considerations
- Proposed budget
- Access issues for construction at site: The ease or difficulty of accessing the building or site with materials and equipment can greatly affect costs of construction. Difficult access can add considerable expense to completing a wall.
- Labor rates and requirements for your situation
- Insurance requirements for construction (general contractor requirements)
- Performance and payment bonds, if required
- State licensing requirements for contractors, if any

3

Constructing a Climbing Wall

As already mentioned, climbing walls can be constructed using a variety of materials and methods. This chapter will focus on basic construction methods that can be broken down into homebuilt wall systems and commercially built wall systems. Construction can involve simple, low-cost systems utilizing methods that people building their own homebuilt walls can use, or it can involve extremely intricate and elaborate steel or shell structures costing a significant amount. This chapter will also provide some general specifications for materials used and space requirements. It will also look at considerations for choosing good wall manufacturers.

Homebuilt Walls

Homebuilt walls tend to be built by the users (figure 3.1) and are generally bouldering wall types. They are usually simple in design and relatively low cost. People often build these for personal use, but some groups, such as camps, schools, or churches, may build walls for use by their participants. All homebuilt walls must be structurally sound. Walls built for group use should meet all pertinent local and state codes as well as CWIG or equivalent industry standards. It is recommended that personal walls also meet the same standards. Homebuilt walls are usually

FIGURE 3.1   Homebuilt wall.

constructed either on preexisting walls or by using a wood frame with plywood sheeting that may be attached to an existing structure (or less commonly may be freestanding).

Preexisting Walls

Climbing holds have been attached to preexisting walls such as a hallway in a school, an unused gymnasium wall, and a concrete retaining wall. Any wall used for such a purpose should be professionally inspected to make sure it is structurally sound and will support the holds and the climbing activity that will take place on it. Holds may be glued on or bolted on.

Glue-On Holds

Glue-on holds are a low-cost method. They can be attached to cement block, brick, concrete, or wood walls. On concrete, brick, and cement block walls, general-purpose epoxy adhesives are often recommended. There are many different ones to choose from. Consult adhesive experts to determine the best adhesive for your wall and hold materials. It is best to glue onto areas without paint to get better adhesion. Blocks of wood cut in various shapes, real rocks of different shapes and sizes, or synthetic commercial holds can all be glued onto a wall. Glue-on holds do have some drawbacks to their use. You are unable to change the holds to create new climbing situations, which limits variety on the wall and soon creates boredom among many users. Glued-on holds also come unglued quite regularly with much use.

Bolt-On Holds

Holds can be bolted directly onto cement block, concrete, and brick walls by drilling holes and using appropriate fasteners for the material drilled. Appropriate fasteners such as five-eighth-inch "short lead shields," into which three-eighth-inch lag screws are inserted, can be obtained at hardware stores and construction material supply houses. Another fastening method uses removable screw-in bolts, which go into threaded sleeves that are epoxied into drilled holes in the concrete, cement block, or brick. Again, consult with construction material suppliers about which fasteners might work best for your job. Three-eighth-inch wood lag screws can be used to attach drilled holds directly onto thick wooden wall materials.

Before holds are attached to a preexisting wall, the builder should decide if he wants or needs to cover the wall with regular or texturized paint. Applying commercially made texturized paint to the wall is highly recommended because it provides for a more realistic surface for footwork. Application methods are similar to those for plywood-surfaced climbing walls (covered later in this chapter).

Wood Frame and Plywood-Covered Walls

A climbing wall constructed with a frame made of two-by-four-inch (5-by-10-centimeter) or larger lumber, onto which three-quarter-inch (1.9 centimeter) GIS (good on one side) four-by-eight-foot (121-by-243-centimeter) plywood sheets are attached, is the most common style of homebuilt climbing wall. This type of wall may be attached to existing wall and ceiling structures or may be a freestanding wall or tower with multiple sides. Freestanding walls and towers often use appropriate-sized telephone poles for the primary vertical supports. Appropriate standards for using telephone poles as support structures should be followed (such as the standards provided by the Association for Challenge Course Technology). Wood-framed, plywood-covered walls can be simple one-angle designs incorporating a slab, vertical, or overhanging face; or they can be elaborate, varied angle, multifaceted designs. You should seek the advice and expertise of engineers and wood construction specialists knowledgeable in how to design and construct wooden walls capable of handling the various stresses, weights, and load forces that may occur during climbing and due to other causes.

Constructing wood-framed, plywood-covered climbing walls requires appropriate fasteners. The plywood sheets are attached using appropriate-sized wood screws, such as two-inch #8 Roberts head or self-tapping Phillips head wood screws, every five inches (12.7 centimeters). You should avoid the weaker drywall screws. The frame is joined together with appropriate-sized bolts, nails, or wood screws as needed. Finally, proper fasteners are needed to secure the frame to existing walls, ceilings, and floors.

Climbing holds are attached to the plywood surface of the wall. Holds may be glued on, but a much more common and functional system is to use three-eighth-inch T-nuts, pallet nuts, or other similar devices, which are sleeves inserted into the plywood (figure 3.2). Climbing holds with a drilled hole through them are attached

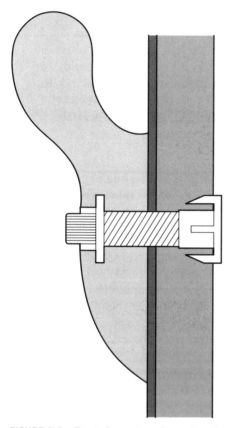

FIGURE 3.2   T-nut sleeve in a plywood wall.

to the inserts using an appropriate three-eighth-inch screw bolt, such as an Allen head cap screw, hex head, or flat head screw bolt, which is screwed into the inserts. This method allows holds to be removed or interchanged at will. The quality of T-nuts and other inserts can vary greatly, so buy the best you can afford to prolong the life of the inserts. You should also check with the hold manufacturer to determine the appropriate bolts to use with their products.

There are a number of factors to consider when selecting the bolts to secure holds to inserts. Allen head cap screws are *much* more expensive to use since they are only available in grade 8. They also come only in nonplated (black) style, which means they should only be used indoors. Hex head screw bolts are relatively cheap because they are available in grade 2 from many hardware supply stores. They are also available in nonplated (indoor use, lower priced) or plated versions (nickel plating being most common, indoor or outdoor use, slightly higher price), enabling them to be used indoors or outdoors.

The layout of T-nuts or similar inserts in the plywood sheets is very important. The more inserts you have in a sheet, the more climbing hold and route options you have. Forty to 60 inserts per 32 square feet (2.9 square meters) is common for tall walls. For bouldering walls, more inserts are used per 32 square feet, with 80 to 120 inserts being common. Tall walls designed for extensive bouldering on the lower 10 to 14 feet (3.0 to 4.2 meters) of the wall will have a higher density of holds in the bouldering area and lesser density above, where only belayed climbing takes place.

Before securing the required four-by-eight-foot plywood sheets on the wall frame, the holes that the inserts will be secured into should be drilled in each plywood sheet. The inserts are then fastened into the holes in the plywood. Make sure you know what size hole needs to be drilled for the inserts being used. For example, three-eighth-inch T-nuts commonly use one-half-inch drilled holes. Although uniform grid patterns of inserts are common on older climbing walls, builders today often recommend more random patterns because they are less repetitive and provide a more varied experience. One company recommends marking an exact grid pattern for the density of inserts desired on each plywood sheet, and then creating a random pattern of drilled holes by drilling individual holes randomly but within five inches (12.7 centimeters) of each marked grid point. The goal is to have uniform insert coverage of each four-by-eight-foot sheet of plywood, but in a random pattern, so that when the wall is constructed the entire wall will be uniformly covered with inserts that are in a random pattern.

As with preexisting walls, the final step before putting the holds on a homebuilt wood-framed, plywood-sheeted wall is to decide whether or not to paint. Although not necessary, it is well worth it to cover the wall with commercial texturized paint that has a high acrylic content. When applying texturized acrylic paint, be sure not to skimp. A common cause of poor results and low durability is to try to extend the amount of surface area a gallon of paint will cover (thus creating too thin a paint layer for good results). Some people creating homebuilt walls attempt to make their own texturized acrylic paint—with less effective results compared to the commercial texturized climbing wall paints. Commonly they add 1 part sand to 10 parts paint volume and then attempt to keep the sand well mixed in the paint by frequent stirrings to prevent the sand from settling out as they paint with a roller. When painting plywood walls where screw-in holds are employed, make sure you don't get the paint in the insert sleeves the holds screw into, because the paint will tend to prevent the holds from being seated properly, causing them to be loose.

After the wall surface is finished, the holds can then be applied. The density of holds can vary greatly, but a common density on walls using inserts is to have twice as many inserts as holds for each plywood sheet. How many holds you need depends on how you will be using your wall, the number of routes and climbers you want to have active at one time, how much money you want to spend, and so on.

Additional Resources for Homebuilt Walls

This book is not intended as a "how to" guide on building a climbing wall; therefore, it does not provide specific plans or details on how to build a homemade wall. Any aspiring climbing facility operator should consult with experienced climbers, legal counsel, and a qualified industry consultant before endeavoring to build a climbing wall. Nevertheless, there are many resources on the Internet, in climbing magazines, and in books that offer specific plans and information that may be helpful as you seek qualified professional advice.

Commercially Built Walls

The interest in utilizing climbing walls by individuals and programs has increased significantly of late. This has fueled an increase in the number of climbing wall manufacturers, methods of construction, and outfitting accessories. Simple homebuilt walls are less expensive to construct and may serve well for the individual looking to work out in the off-season at home, or for programs with limited resources whose goals and objectives can be met with simple climbing walls. Everything being equal, though, most programs and commercial ventures wanting to utilize a climbing wall will most likely be better served in the long run by using the services of commercial climbing wall designers and manufacturers (figure 3.3).

Climbing Wall Manufacturers

Many commercial climbing wall manufacturers operate in the United States both regionally and nationwide. They vary from very small to very large operations. Other manufacturers can be found who operate in North America and around the world. A good place to start finding possible vendors is the Internet and climbing-oriented magazines. You might also be able to get a listing of climbing wall manufacturers who are active CWA members by contacting the CWA. As mentioned before, the previous work of vendors should be checked thoroughly to help you find a manufacturer whose product, services, and quality will satisfy your needs.

FIGURE 3.3   Commercially built wall.
© Nicros

Construction Methods

Commercial climbing wall designers and manufacturers have a variety of construction materials and methods to choose from when designing and constructing climbing walls. The construction method or mix of methods you choose should be based on such factors as budgetary considerations, location, aesthetics desired, clientele to be served, and how realistic to nature you want the wall to be. Some common construction methods include basic wood panel systems with bolt-on holds; interchangeable modular prefabricated polymer cement panels with three-dimensional features and bolt-on holds; concrete shells; and precast special concrete (some form of fiberglass reinforced concrete) systems utilizing molds of real rock. Commercial walls may make use of preexisting walls onto which holds and texturing are attached; may include wall frames of steel or wood that are attached to existing walls, floors, and ceilings; or may be freestanding wood- or steel-framed structures.

Wood Panels

Wood panel systems, available with or without textured surfaces, use frames of wood or, more commonly, welded steel (which is more expensive). Plywood panels are attached to the framing and are then covered with a special surface-texturing material such as texturized paint or thin, flat coatings of special cements to provide a more rocklike surface. The

FIGURE 3.4   Highly faceted wood panel system.

panels are drilled for T-nuts or similar inserts to which modular bolt-on holds can be attached or removed. These panels should have uniform coverage of the panel surface with inserts located in a random pattern. Wood panel systems can be simple one-angle designs or highly faceted, multiple-angle, multiple-feature structures (figure 3.4). The surface of wood panel systems is flat in nature, and the screw-on holds provide the means for upward movement. This type of construction tends to be the least expensive commercial climbing wall construction method.

Polymer Cement Panels

Another construction method involves premade interlocking panels (with bolt-on attachable holds) made of polymer cement. The panels are three-dimensional and are carved to provide more rocklike features. They are highly textured and have a multitude of modular bolt-on hold placements per panel. More elaborate panels have natural holds carved into the surface of the panels to allow climbing without the need to use bolt-on holds, though most use a combination of carved and bolt-on holds. A steel frame is commonly used (onto which the panels are attached to provide the climbing surface). Most companies have a large selection of different panel surface configurations to add variety to a wall. The panels are often interchangeable, but in real life very few programs with this type of climbing wall change the panels once they are on the wall. It is a lot of work to change the panels. However, if a panel becomes defective, it can be replaced.

Concrete Shells

For concrete shell climbing wall structures, a thin shell of sculptable special reinforced concrete is applied onto a structural steel frame. The concrete can be made into many shapes and climbing features. The surface may be carved to create features such as finger cracks, flakes, pockets, jam cracks, and so on. Generally, a combination of carved natural hold features and bolt-on holds are incorporated into the wall. The more carved features the wall has, the more expensive it will be. Shell concrete structures can be made to include a greater variety of shapes and features compared to three-dimensional cement panel and wood panel climbing walls.

Precast Real Rock Molds

The most realistic and rocklike climbing walls tend to be made from molds of real rock using special resinous reinforced cements. Varying molded shapes are attached to a steel subframe in a manner that eliminates seams and creates a real-life cliff face, or boulder, which can be climbed on directly like real rock (figure 3.5). The surfaces are also suitable for bolt-on hold inserts. You can usually have routes of varying difficulty just by specifying that climbers use only the bolt-on holds, only the natural surface holds, or a combination of both. Rock-molded cement tall walls and bouldering walls are very aesthetically pleasing and are often more realistic climbing surfaces. More realistic footwork possibilities are a nice advantage of this type of wall construction as well.

FIGURE 3.5 **Precast real rock molds.**
© Nicros

Wall Specifications

Climbing walls should be designed and constructed to meet or exceed all applicable local, state, and federal building codes and standards. They should also comply with applicable current climbing wall industry design, engineering, and construction standards set for your location, such as the CWIG standards for climbing walls in the United States. In the United States, you should contact the CWA (Climbing Wall Association) for up-to-date information on applicable climbing wall industry standards for wall design, engineering, and construction; and to find out how you can obtain current standards. If constructing a climbing wall as part of a challenge course using telephone poles for the vertical support structure, you may also want to consult the ACCT (Association for Challenge Course Technology) standards available through the ACCT. Any commercial climbing wall designer, builder, or manufacturer of merit should build their climbing walls to current applicable standards. People building private homebuilt walls should also consult and build to applicable climbing wall standards for their location. The following are some common specifications for miscellaneous climbing wall aspects. Please consult industry standards for a complete listing of specifications.

Anchors

CWIG standards indicate that all anchors must be capable of withstanding loads of 4,400 pounds (1,995 kilograms) of force in multiple directions. Anchors may be top-rope upper belay running anchors, lead-climbing protection anchors, or belay floor anchors.

Top-Rope Top Running Anchors

Top-roping tall walls tend to use either three-inch (7.6-centimeter) diameter steel bars anchored to the top of individual climbing routes, or two UIAA- or ASTM-approved lead protection bolts with hangers placed side by side to which quickdraws or steel chains with locking carabiners or one-half-inch rapid links are attached. The belay rope runs from the climber up over the belay bar and back down to the belayer, or it is clipped into both quickdraw locking carabiners or rapid links and then goes back down to the belayer.

Lead-Climbing Protection Anchors

Lead-climbing protection anchors should be properly spaced up the wall to prevent a falling lead climber from hitting the floor or taking long falls. Lead climbers should also be required to clip each bolt provided (in order of ascent) to reduce the length of falls and to attempt to prevent Z-clipping. Z-clipping occurs when an ascending lead climber passes by a protection anchor, clips his rope to a protection anchor above, and then clips the belay rope coming from his harness tie-in to the protection anchor he passed. This creates a hazardous situation because excessive rope drag (friction) makes it difficult for the climber to ascend and will increase the distance of a fall if the climber continues to ascend. Strategically placing resting holds from which it is easy to clip each protection anchor as a climber reaches it helps to prevent a climber from passing a protection anchor without clipping it. The height of the first protection anchor from the floor should be appropriate to the situation, with a maximum height of between 10 and 14 feet (3.0 and 4.2 meters) commonly recommended. CWIG standards recommend that spacing between protection anchors be no greater than six feet six and three-quarters inches (about 200 centimeters). A particularly difficult route might necessitate closer placement of protection points than might be required on easier routes. Special care is needed in locating lead-climbing protection anchors on overhanging routes to prevent excessive swings back into the wall below the overhang or ceiling.

On some older climbing walls, lead-climbing protection anchors may be necessary on portions of top-rope tall wall routes that are greatly overhanging, such as a ceiling, to limit backswing distances that might cause a climber to swing into a belayer, into other climbers on the wall, or into other portions of the wall. On top-rope routes requiring this kind of protection, the belay rope coming from the climber on the ground is prethreaded through the protection anchors up the route and over the upper belay anchor (then back down to the belayer). As the climber ascends, he unclips from the protection anchor quickdraws as he passes them. When the climber has finished the route and is being lowered, he should clip the belay rope above the tie-in point of his harness back into each protection anchor as he descends. This prepares the route for a new top-rope climber. It is recommended today that top-rope tall walls be designed to eliminate the need for back-protecting routes.

Floor Anchors

Floor anchors provided for belaying purposes should be properly located away from the landing zone for the route being belayed. Eight feet (243 centimeters) back is often given as an adequate distance. Refer to "Floor Anchors" in chapter 2 (page 25) for a detailed discussion.

Bouldering Wall Heights

The maximum height commonly recommended for bouldering walls is 10 to 14 feet (3.0 to 4.2 meters), with 10 feet being the most common. However, the age of participants affects how high they should be allowed to boulder. One climbing wall manufacturer recommends the following heights: 5 feet (152 centimeters) for kindergarten-age children, 7 feet (213 centimeters) for elementary-age children, and 10 feet (3 meters) for high-school-age and adult participants. On tall walls incorporating bouldering on the lower section of the wall, a painted horizontal line is often put on the wall to indicate the high point allowed for the hands while climbing without a belay rope. Other methods for attempting to limit the height of boulderers include allowing the boulderer's feet to be no higher than the spotter's head, or placing a horizontal line on the traverse wall above which the boulderer's feet may not go. The latter is often seen on traverse walls for young children.

Landing Zones

All climbing walls, whether bouldering or tall walls, need to have impact-lessening surfaces appropriately located under each route. Exact specifications are difficult to provide because they are highly dependent on the nature of the climb and situation, and on manufacturer recommendations. You should follow the manufacturer's recommendations for depth and distance of landing surface material required for your specific bouldering, top-roping, and lead-climbing heights. Refer to "Landing Surface" in chapter 2 (page 34) for additional information.

Cost Considerations

It is beyond the scope of this book to indicate how much money a wall will cost. Consulting commercial climbing wall manufacturers is an effective method for determining how much your wall will cost to construct and maintain. They should be able to help you produce a design brief based on your needs, desires, facility constraints, location, the number and nature of the clientele to be served, budget constraints, construction method desired, and so forth. The following are three examples of climbing walls with their approximate costs. These examples (figures 3.6, 3.7, and 3.8) may help you understand what you might get for a low-, medium-, and high-cost project.

Summary

From reading this chapter, you can see that constructing a climbing wall requires numerous decisions to be made and numerous steps to be followed. We close this chapter by offering the steps generally followed to take the initial design and bring it to reality and operation. These steps include the following:

- Develop a design, ideally with the assistance of professional designers and licensed structural engineers who have significant experience in the design and construction of climbing walls and who are familiar with climbing wall industry standards for your location.

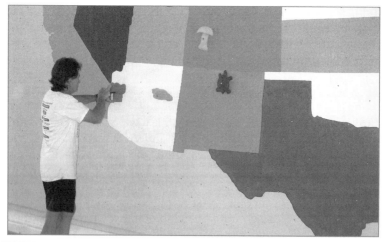

FIGURE 3.6 Lower-cost example—middle school climbing wall (about $3000).

FIGURE 3.7 Moderate-cost example—community center project (about $12000).
© Nicros

FIGURE 3.8 High-cost example—upper-end university climbing wall project (about $50000).
© Nicros

- Contact local building and planning departments to determine what building requirements, codes, and permits you will have to comply with, if any. If a climbing wall is to be part of a larger building design, the building permit is inclusive of all aspects of the building, including the climbing wall.
- Select a licensed construction contractor if the designer is not also the builder.
- Develop your project's blueprints in compliance with all applicable codes and industry standards.
- Obtain all necessary permits. Formal approval of the project by a licensed engineer is often necessary to allow occupancy.
- Build the structure, including all hardware, anchor points, and landing zone surfaces.
- Have the site inspected by the local building department as required.
- Obtain an occupancy permit if required.
- Outfit the wall.
- Train staff.
- Provide ongoing, periodic in-service staff training while in operation.
- Perform necessary wall and equipment checks, maintenance, and record keeping.

Selecting Climbing Equipment

Building a climbing wall is much like building a house. So much time and effort are put into building it that once it is completed you simply want to sit back and enjoy it. We all know that this is not going to be the case. Once a climbing wall is built, attention must turn to adding furnishings (i.e., equipment). Chapter 4 will focus on specialized climbing wall equipment and its maintenance and care.

Specialized Climbing Wall Equipment

Climbing safety equipment to be used on a climbing wall should be approved for that purpose by the CE/UIAA (Committee for European Normalization/Union International Des Associations d'Alpinisme) or the ASTM (American Society for Test and Measurements). Climbing equipment normally needed to outfit a climbing wall includes, but is not limited to, belay ropes, sit harnesses, belay devices, carabiners, quickdraws, rapid links, slings, bolt hangers, climbing shoes, rappel devices, and helmets.

Belay Ropes

Belay ropes are an important part of the safety system on tall climbing walls. There are many manufacturers of climbing ropes to select from, so you should shop around to find the ropes that meet the dynamic qualities, handling characteristics (ease of use when moving the rope through belay devices and stopping a falling climber), and durability required. The CWIG standards indicated the use of UIAA-approved single dynamic belay ropes. This holds true today as well. Dynamic belay ropes are designed to reduce impact forces when arresting a fall by elongating (stretching) a limited amount. Thus they reduce the impact forces on the climbing wall structure, anchors, and other parts of the belay system, as well as on the climber. Walls built to CWIG standards are designed to handle the stresses and loads that occur when stopping the fall of a belayed climber with dynamic belay ropes. The use of static line ropes is not recommended unless your wall is specifically designed to handle the higher stress they put onto the wall and anchors during a catch. Static line ropes are designed with low-elongation characteristics that impart higher impact forces on the climber, the climbing wall structure, and the anchors when a fall is stopped by the belay system, as compared to dynamic belay ropes. "Gym-line" belay ropes, that is, dynamic belay ropes designed specifically for climbing walls, are seeing more use as an alternative to single dynamic belay ropes. They have good durability and fall between dynamic ropes and static line in elongation qualities. Dynamic belay ropes that are 10.5 to 11 millimeters in diameter are the standard for strength and durability, but smaller diameter single dynamic belay ropes are adequate as well if approved by the manufacturer. A drawback to smaller diameter single dynamic belay ropes is that they must be replaced more often due to quicker wear and capacity to handle fewer falls. The use of smaller diameter dynamic belay ropes may also require properly sized belay devices to provide the necessary friction to brake a fall satisfactorily. This is true of larger diameter ropes as well. Belay devices must be matched to the ropes you are planning to use to get the best combination of friction, stopping ability, and ease of rope movement through the device during rope uptake, catching, and lowering.

Sit Harnesses

All sit harnesses approved by the CE/UIAA are acceptable for climbing wall use (figure 4.1). Most climbing wall programs utilize multipurpose harnesses with a waist belt and leg loop combination. Very few climbing programs today use wide webbing that allows climbers to tie their own harnesses (swami-belts). Swami-belts take practice to tie, can be hazardous if improperly fitted (may inhibit breathing or crimp the rib cage), require frequent inspection and adjustments, and are downright uncomfortable after climbing for a while. Harnesses vary considerably in price, comfort, and ease of use. You should shop around and try out various styles. Belay loops are becoming standard on harnesses and should be used by

FIGURE 4.1   Sit harness.

climbing wall operators. Sit harnesses should be used according to the manufacturer's recommendations. Proper fit is critical to guarantee the harness stays in place and distributes forces properly in a fall. Most harnesses require that the waist buckle be doubled-back, but there are some harnesses that utilize other systems. Climbing wall supervisors, staff, and participants must be familiar with the intricacies and special features of any harnesses used. They should know how to put on, adjust, and inspect the harnesses for wear, and they should know where to tie into each type of harness used. If your climbing wall is used primarily for group instruction, you may want to consider institutional style, one size fits all, adjustable sit harnesses as a means to save money and streamline the harness-fitting and instruction process. When using harnesses of varying sizes, it is necessary to buy more harnesses than the number of people to be served since you do not know what sizes you will need. Varying size harnesses, however, do often provide a more comfortable fit for clients. Whether using "one size fits all" or varying size harnesses, it is convenient to have all your harnesses be the same model to avoid confusion on how to tie into the harnesses or how to belay off them.

Climbing wall programs have to decide what age children they will allow to climb on belay. Most children below the age of 10—and some adults with body shapes lacking large enough hip-to-waist dimensions to prevent securely fitted seat harness waist belts from sliding over their hips—need to use full-body harnesses to get a proper fit. Check with manufacturers about their recommendations for when a full-body seat harness versus a sit harness should be used.

Belay Devices

Though there are a large number of belay devices on the market, most belay devices for climbing walls come in two basic styles: standard belay friction devices and automatic (auto-belay) belay devices. When human belayers are used to belay a climber, it is recommended that a CE/UIAA standard belay friction device be used in conjunction with the belay loop of a belayer's sit harness and locking carabiners (figure 4.2). Standard belay friction devices are generally passive devices that require the belayer to physically control rope movement with his brake hand at all times to enable the device to lock on the rope. Standard friction belay devices come in a variety of styles. Slotted, tube style belay devices are most popular today, but some slotted plate style devices are still in service. Figure eight style belay and rappel devices can be used as well, but these devices are less commonly used for belaying on climbing walls today because they tend to impart a twist to the belay rope, particularly when lowering climbers; this makes for kinky, knotted ropes for the belayer to deal with after a few climbers have gone on the same rope. A few standard belay friction devices, such as the Grigri, have a backup self-locking feature that will stop a rope sliding through them if the belayer accidentally takes his brake hand off the rope during a fall. You should note that these belay devices are not automatic belay devices, and they require the use of the belayer's brake hand at all times to be used properly. A number of other friction belay devices also work but cannot easily be pigeonholed into one of the above categories. Refer to appendix B for a partial listing of standard friction belay devices and their manufacturers. Please note that the authors do not recommend one belay device over others. You should research and try out belay devices to find ones that are right for your specific situation and needs.

FIGURE 4.2   Belay friction device.

Automatic belay device systems (auto-belays) require no human belayer involvement. Most commonly found on rock-climbing wall mobile amusements, auto-belays use a cable (attached to the climber's sit harness) that retracts into the device at the top of the wall route as the climber ascends, locks on any rapid descent (fall), and will slowly lower the climber when she wants to descend. Depending on the type of device, auto-belays tend to be somewhat expensive, but they do allow for more climbers to climb in a specified period of time. The U.S. Consumer Product Safety Commission (see appendix B) recommends that auto-belay manufacturer recommendations be followed to use these products correctly. They also provide some additional safety guidelines for the use of auto-belays with climbing walls. This book focuses primarily on the use of human belayers and standard belay friction devices. In most climbing wall programs, particularly educational programs, the intent is for the participants to be highly involved in all aspects of climbing, not just the climbing itself. The belayer–climber relationship is an important aspect within the educational use of climbing walls.

Proper connection and skill are required to use any belay device correctly. Wall operators should try out different models of the type of belay device they are planning to use prior to purchasing them. Devices vary considerably. Determine which devices offer the best combination of braking power, ease of rope movement, and easily controlled lowering action for the ropes that will be used. Program goals and operation considerations should also be taken into account when deciding on which type of belay device to select.

Carabiners

Locking and nonlocking CE/UIAA-approved carabiners are used on climbing walls. Locking carabiners in either an oval or D-shape configuration are used to connect parts of the belay and climbing systems together. There are a number of different locking carabiner options that can be used, including auto-locking, twist lock, and screw-gate models. Common connections using locking carabiners include belay ropes and belay devices to seat harness belay loops; belayers to belay floor anchor systems; quickdraws to protection anchors (one-half-inch steel rapid link is approved here also); rappel devices with inserted ropes to the belay/rappel loop of a harness; belay ropes to double point top-rope upper belay anchors (one-half-inch steel rapid links also approved here); and the climber connecting his belay rope at the top of the climb to double point anchors to be lowered back to the ground by the belayer. Auto-locking carabiners are fast becoming the connection method of choice, especially for connecting the belay device with attached belay rope to the belayer's harness belay loop. These carabiners use a spring-loaded gate that automatically locks closed when the opened gate is released, and they require a twist and slide movement or a push of a button to unlock the gate. They tend to be the most secure method of locking the gate of a carabiner to prevent the accidental unclipping of the belay rope or belay device from the belayer's harness. Even so, make sure to squeeze check the gate whenever using a locking carabiner of any type (dirt could interfere with proper closure or it might become sticky, which can lead to an open gate and a hazardous situation).

Nonlocking carabiners are generally used for the outer end of lead climb protection anchor quickdraws. Carabiners can be made of either aluminum or steel. Steel carabiners are recommended in locations that will receive a lot of rope friction, such as lowering-off points of double point anchor top-rope anchors. Steel is much more durable and will save money in the long run. Aluminum is better in low-wear points since aluminum locking carabiners are less expensive. One-half-inch steel rapid links are even less expensive and may be used in areas where more permanent connections are desired, such as attaching a quickdraw to a lead climb anchor or the lowering-off point on double point top-rope anchors.

It is difficult to specify exactly how many locking and nonlocking carabiners a climbing wall may require. Each wall has different needs. A simple traversing bouldering wall may not require any carabiners, while an elaborate tall wall designed for lead climbing and top-roping will require a significant number of both. Most top-roping-only tall walls usually use locking carabiners. A top-roping tall wall using steel bars as the top-rope running anchors may only require one locking carabiner per belayer per route in operation, plus some auxiliary locking ones for maintenance or rescue operations. It is when lead climbing is included that nonlocking carabiners tend to be included in the mix. The size of the tall wall also plays a large part in the number of carabiners required. More routes means more carabiners are required. Once a wall is designed, you can then determine the approximate number of connectors needed to hook the parts of the system together (based on the number of routes operating, number of lead-climbing routes set up, use of floor anchors for belayers, type of top-rope running anchors used, maintenance requirements, rescue operation plans, and so on).

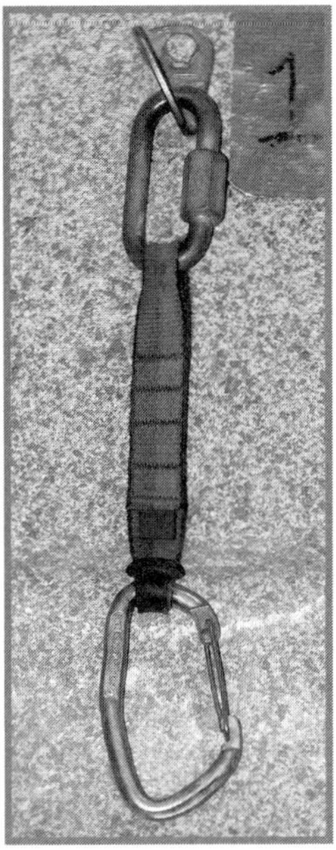

Quickdraws

A quickdraw consists of either a locking carabiner or a one-half-inch steel rapid link onto which a short sewn sling is attached, with the other end of the sling having a non-locking carabiner attached. The quickdraw's locking carabiner or rapid link is secured to the protection anchor so that the gate is locked closed and is in a downward position (figure 4.3). Normally the quickdraw slings are made from sewn nylon, spectra, or similar material capable of holding at least 4,400 pounds (1,995 kilograms) of force if used in anchors.

FIGURE 4.3   Quickdraw.

One-Half-Inch Steel Rapid Links

One-half-inch steel rapid links (figure 4.4) should not be confused with cold shuts (figure 4.5), which

FIGURE 4.4   Rapid links.

should not be used on climbing walls for any attachment and safety aspects. For more information on one-half-inch steel rapid links, refer to "Carabiners" earlier in this chapter.

FIGURE 4.5   Cold shuts.

Slings

Slings are pieces of webbing (nylon, spectra, or similar material) normally sewn into sling (oval) form and capable of holding 4,400 pounds (1,995 kilograms) if used as part of the belay system, such as anchoring the belayer. Daisy chains are specially sewn slings that have multiple carabiner attachment points sewn into the sling.

Stainless Steel Protection Bolt Hangers

CE/UIAA-approved bolt hangers should be used on all lead climb protection anchors and double point anchor top-rope belay upper anchors.

Climbing Shoes

Special climbing shoes are not necessary for use on a climbing wall, but they do increase the climbing performance of participants. Any nonmarking athletic shoe will work, with white soles being more suitable than black. However, most climbing wall programs supply specialty climbing shoes to participants who do not have their own. For renting to participants with a wide variety of climbing skill levels, it is best to go with a general, all-around climbing shoe. Consult manufacturers of climbing shoes to see what they have to offer and recommend. We recommend specialty climbing shoes because they will enhance the climbers' ability to use their feet on small edgy holds, provide better friction on holds, and provide better feel (sensitivity) for footwork on holds. Basically, they allow you to climb better. But if you can't afford to have shoes available for your participants, it is still well worth climbing with other shoes. If participants are climbing with nonclimbing shoes, they can make the shoes perform better by lacing them tightly, particularly in the front of the shoe. Selecting nonclimbing shoes that have little sole sticking out past the shoe itself also aids in using them to climb.

Rappel Devices

Some climbing wall programs incorporate rappelling into their wall activities. Educational programs who have tall climbing walls and who teach climbing with the intent to transfer the skills of climbing to outdoor environments are the most likely to have walls with this capability designed and constructed. Even tall walls without rappelling opportunities will most likely require at least one descending device as part of the program's equipment inventory. The device may be needed for use by staff during routine maintenance activities or to provide some rescue capabilities where descending from the top of the wall is necessary and other methods of descent (such as a power lift) are not available. Rappel devices are usually figure eight rappel/belay style or standard belay friction tube or plate style devices that are designed for rappelling as well. As with all equipment, you should read and understand the manufacturer's recommendations for proper use and application of their devices. Some belay devices are suitable for rappelling and vice versa. Devices that tend not to impart twists into the rope are preferred. Tube or plate style standard belay friction devices usually do not impart as much twist into rappel ropes as figure eight styles do.

Helmets

Required helmet use on climbing walls varies greatly. Although everyone agrees that helmets are a great idea, they can be uncomfortable and not always necessary indoors. Helmets should always be used for climbing outdoors. Some programs mandate helmets for all climbing activities (particularly school and institutional programs); others do not require helmet use at anytime. Some climbing wall programs allow participants to climb without a helmet if the climber signs a helmet waiver. (See appendix A for a sample waiver.) You will have to decide based on legal counsel, insurance considerations, risk management planning, and standards by which you are operating whether helmets should be used on your wall. The potential for head injury is greater for lead-climbing activities than for top-roping or bouldering, but no climbing activity is completely free of the possibility of head injuries. Remember, it is always safer to climb with a CE/UIAA-approved *climbing* helmet on your head. If providing helmets for participants, climbing wall programs are best served by using comfortable fitting, easily adjusted helmets, which will fit different-sized heads properly. Using helmets that are adjustable for size saves a program money in the long run because the program does not have to buy as many to fit the clientele served. Nonadjustable helmets require varying sizes to fit different head sizes, and you must have a significant number more than the number of climbers actively climbing at one time (to fit the potential number of different head sizes). The number of adjustable helmets a climbing wall operation needs on hand is usually based on the number of climbers climbing at the same time, plus a few extra in case of breakage. Using helmets that are not fitted properly is not recommended. Follow the manufacturer's recommendations for proper fitting requirements.

Nonclimbing Equipment for the Climbing Wall

A few pieces of equipment that are not specifically related to climbing are necessary, or in some cases just convenient, for the operation of a climbing wall. A toolbox is recommended and should include at a minimum any special tools required for attaching and tightening the type of holds to be used on the wall surface; pliers to open up stubborn screw lock gates on carabiners, and so forth; a crescent wrench or box wrenches of appropriate size to open and close rapid link sleeves; a sharp knife or other appropriate cutting implement; and some electrical tape. Another important item is a complete first aid kit, which should be onsite and located in a strategic spot. Some items that are nice to have on hand but are not usually absolutely necessary include an electrical rope burner to cut ropes and webbing and to melt nylon rope and sling ends; ladders of appropriate size for your needs; buckets; scrub brushes; biodegradable soap for cleaning holds periodically; a wash sink; and a vacuum cleaner for the floor and landing surfaces if not made of loose materials.

Equipment Maintenance and Care

All climbing equipment should be maintained, cared for, and retired or replaced according to the manufacturers' suggested guidelines. These may vary considerably among manufacturers. This section describes some general considerations on the topic.

Belay Ropes

Belay ropes serve as the climbers' lifeline in the event of a fall. As such they need to be frequently checked for proper condition. Written procedures should be implemented and followed that include frequent and routine inspections of belay ropes for conditions that may necessitate the removal of a suspect rope from service. Determine a routine schedule for when belay ropes in use are inspected, and have a reporting system that can be used to identify problems and remove suspect belay ropes. Some climbing wall programs check the condition of the belay ropes at the start of each day and at the end of the day's operation, and also whenever a belay rope sustains a severe fall.

Belay ropes need to be checked for wear on an ongoing basis. Common ways to inspect a belay rope include feeling the rope by running it through the fingers and visually inspecting the rope for signs of significant wear. Significant cuts and nicks in the sheath of the rope exposing the core, changes in the core of the rope (flat spots, thinner spots, or softer spots), and unusual stiffness or softness in parts of the rope should be further evaluated for possible weakening of the rope. Severe falls, such as those that may occur in lead climbing, should also trigger evaluation of the belay rope for problems.

General Rope Care

Rope care is an ongoing process involving staff and clientele. You must educate your staff and clientele never to stand on the ropes because this may damage them. Ropes that are left hanging up from the top-rope running anchors between sessions should be tied up when not in use if the potential exists for them to be stepped on. This can be done by daisy chaining the lower portion of the hanging belay ropes so that they are not touching the floor, or by pulling the ropes up in the air along the wall by using auxiliary ropes. Ropes not in service on the wall should be coiled properly or placed in appropriately sized storage bags and stored in a cool, dry place, out of the UV rays of direct sunlight, which tends to weaken ropes over time. Ropes must also be kept away from any chemicals, particularly acids, and away from any heat sources, which can melt the ropes. You must also make sure that wet or damp ropes are completely dry before being stored away.

Periodic inspection of ropes for wear is important. You must also check out unusual signs of rope wear immediately and try to determine the cause. If a rope is wearing in one spot, and that rope is always used on the same route, try to evaluate where on the wall or the belay system it is occurring, and why it is wearing as it is. Often the location of a hold, how the rope is being belayed, or where the climbers are being lowered may be the cause. Make changes to prevent the wear from continuing. One potential source of wear is the rope-connecting hardware. Regularly check the rope-connecting and anchor hardware for nicks and sharp edges that may wear the rope. Another source of wear in one spot is the tie-in points at the end of the rope. Every so often, you should switch the ends you are tying into. Periodically switching the end of the rope you tie into helps extend the life of the rope by not focusing all the stress and wear of tying in on one end of the rope only, or only at the belay side of the rope. Wear is spread out somewhat by doing so, rather than concentrating it in certain spots.

Finally, you should wash ropes periodically when they seem dirty—check your hands. If the belayers' hands are getting excessively black while belaying, it is time to wash the rope. Washing dirty belay ropes helps to get any grit and dirt out of the sheath so it does not work its way into the core and shorten the life of the belay rope through increased wear. It also extends the life of your belay devices and associated carabiners by reducing excessive wear on the devices due to grit and dirt particles in the rope. Follow the manufacturer's recommendations for when and how to wash their belay ropes. One common method is to place the uncoiled rope in a large laundry bag that can be closed, flush out any old soapy water left in a tumble style washing machine, then fill the machine with clean cold water without soap (especially detergents) and wash the rope within the bag. Hang it up to dry in a cool, dry place indoors until it is completely dry.

Retiring or Replacing Ropes

There is no set formula for retiring a belay rope except the maxim "when in doubt, throw it out." Belay ropes should be inspected and retired based on the manufacturer's recommendations. One manufacturer, Beal Ropes, suggests that you expect a maximum of three years under normal use and with no out-of-the-ordinary wear going on. Belay ropes experiencing several hours of daily use, such as occurs in many climbing gyms, may require much shorter time schedules. Rope inspections play a significant role in when to retire a rope. Some guidelines for early rope retirement and inspection include the following:

- Retire a rope if any cut or wear exposes the sheath.
- Retire a rope if significant contact with a chemical, especially acids, occurs.
- Retire a rope that has significant wearing of the sheath.
- Retire a rope with glazed sheaths from heat or rapid rappelling.
- Ropes that have held a severe leader fall should be suspect and closely evaluated.
- Significant changes in the feel of the core of the rope in relation to the rest of the rope, such as flat spots, soft spots, or an extremely stiff portion, should be retired. Beal Ropes indicates that ropes start out supple and easy to use, gradually become stiffer and less supple over the length of the rope, and eventually go limp and soft again, which is a sign to retire the rope.

Rope logs should be used to record the manufacturing date of the rope and when the rope was put into service. Some programs also attempt to record the number of hours of use each rope receives per day, week, and month and the number of hard falls the rope has sustained, but this is extremely difficult to do effectively. This information can be used to help determine when to retire a rope when coupled with the all-important ongoing inspections of the ropes. Some programs have their ropes numbered on one end so they can be tracked. A sample rope inspection log can be found in appendix A. Retired ropes should be cut into smaller lengths, and each portion should have the ends taped or painted black (a nationally recognized symbol for retired ropes no longer suitable for belay or other safety use) to indicate retirement.

Magazines focusing on rock climbing are good sources for information on dynamic belay rope care, use, and inspection. For a partial listing of related resources, please refer to appendix B.

Carabiners

Carabiners should be visually and manually inspected for any signs of cracks, wearing, or sharp edges. Check the gates to see if they close and open smoothly and completely. Check the locking mechanism on the gates of locking carabiners for proper function and smoothness. Sticky gates can be lubricated with an appropriate dry lubricant designed not to weaken synthetic dynamic belay ropes. Check with the manufacturer to determine appropriate lubricants. A number of lubricants are available that are usually graphite, Teflon, or silicon based. Ideally, dust and dirt should not stick to the lubricant used. Retire any carabiner that is dropped from high up (especially onto hard surfaces), shows significant wear (obvious grooving from rope) through the surface of the carabiner, has malfunctioning locking mechanisms, or has gates that do not close all the way. Please refer to appendix B for sources of information.

Belay Devices and Rappel Devices

Belay and rappel devices normally require little maintenance. They should be replaced if they are dropped from significant heights, if they show obvious grooving of the metal surfaces, or if the keeper wire bails are frayed (though these can be replaced). You should follow the manufacturer's instructions for use and inspect the devices regularly.

Climbing Shoes

A program's climbing shoes, if used by more than one person, should have the inside of the shoes sprayed with an antifungal/germicidal spray that leaves no residue after each use, and should be stored in an area where they can air dry. Shoes that show signs of being close to wearing through the rand (side of shoe) or sole of the shoe, and any shoe showing delamination, should be pulled from service until they can be resoled or replaced. Resoling before the rand is worn through is important because this is a much less expensive resoling job than if you wait until the rand is worn through as well as the sole. Recently the cost of some climbing shoes has become low enough that some programs are finding it more economical to buy new replacement shoes rather than have them resoled. You need to decide which method is best for your program based on the shoes you are using.

Helmets

Climbing helmets used by more than one person must be sprayed on the inside of the helmet with antilice and antibacterial sprays after each use. Any helmet dropped from a significant height should be retired, as should ones showing crushed liners or cracked shells.

Slings and Quickdraws (Sewn Webbing and Webbing Used for Anchors)

Because slings and draws are made from nylon and other synthetic materials similar to ropes, the general care guidelines for ropes can also apply to slings and draws. They should be checked for significant cuts and signs of wear. Retire any slings or draws showing significant wear or cuts, and any that have caught or sustained a severe fall. Keep records of when they were manufactured and put into service. All retired webbing should be cut up or destroyed so it cannot be used.

Sit Harnesses

As with dynamic belay ropes and webbing, sit harnesses are made of nylon or other synthetic materials. Many of the general care guidelines for ropes apply to sit harnesses. Sit harnesses should be inspected frequently for significant wear and abuses necessitating retirement, including the following:

- Significant cuts or nicks, especially in the tie-in and waist belt areas.
- Improper functioning of any safety buckles.
- Glazed areas damaged by heat sources and excessive friction. (To increase the life of the tie-in area of harnesses, it is good to slowly weave the belay rope through the tie-in area when tying in and taking the rope off the harness. This reduces friction wear in this area.)
- Having been subjected to a severe fall or catch.
- Significant contact with chemicals or acids.
- Excessive exposure to ultraviolet light over time.
- Significant changes in the feel of the nylon.

Follow the manufacturer's recommendations for the care, inspection, and retirement of sit harnesses. Two years of weekend use is often given as the average life of a sit harness when not subjected to additional or unusual abuses. If a sit harness has frayed webbing ends, the ends should be remelted to prevent unraveling or splitting, and to make it easier to secure harness ends in buckles as required.

Attachable Holds

All bolt-on holds should be inspected periodically for cracks, stripped threads, flaking, and flexing. Retire any holds and attachment bolts showing such signs. It is a good idea to periodically clean holds to remove chalk, shoe rubber particles, and dirt residue (thus returning the holds to their original feel and texture). Follow the manufacturer's directions for cleaning their holds. Destroy any retired holds so they cannot be accidentally used.

Belay Anchors and Lead Climb Protection Anchors (Superstuds, Coldstuds, and Belay Bars)

Anchors should be inspected for significant wear and proper attachment to the wall and substructure. Any significant wear in the surface of anchors or looseness that can't be corrected needs to be addressed by knowledgeable professionals. Follow manufacturer directions for retiring these items. Belay anchors and lead anchors usually require professional replacement. Bolt hangers should be inspected for wear and cracking. Replace any showing significant wear or grooving. Replace any bolt hanger system where the hanger cannot be tightened to prevent movement (spinning) of the hanger.

Equipment Storage

Equipment should be stored in a secure, dry location that allows efficient organization and access to the equipment. Good ventilation for stored equipment allows items to dry if damp and avoids trapping moisture in the equipment. Ropes and harnesses should be hung so they can be easily inspected. (Ropes should not be hung by a single strand.) Climbing shoes and helmets are best stored on shelves so they can be easily sprayed when needed. Harnesses should be stored by size and are often hung up in bundles using rope pieces to hook the harnesses together. Ideally, each piece of equipment should be numbered and identified for logistical and inventory purposes. Equipment that comes in different sizes, such as climbing shoes, helmets (if nonadjustable), and harnesses (if nonadjustable), should have the size clearly marked on them. These items should be stored in a manner that is organized to allow easy size identification, access, and efficient controlled distribution of the equipment when being given out to clients. This is particularly important for operations providing rentals of equipment. Finally, any storage containers should be labeled with what they contain to increase the efficiency of locating desired equipment.

Equipment Purchase and Replacement

All climbing equipment used to outfit a climbing wall should meet appropriate industry standards; for example, CE/UIAA-certified equipment for climbing and fall protection use. You should note that not all manufacturers of suitable climbing wall equipment apply for CE/UIAA certification for their products in the United States. Quality equipment may be purchased from many sources. Shop around to get the best prices. Schools, recreation programs, and commercial operations can often get significant discounts through retailers or even wholesalers of climbing equipment. Bulk orders of equipment often provide a lower item cost. Direct savings can be incurred at times by dealing with companies or wholesalers rather than local shops. Climbing ropes can be purchased in 600-foot (182-meter) spools at significant savings over purchasing outdoor-oriented lead-climbing ropes that come in standard lengths. They can then be cut to the exact length required. See appendix B for some sources of climbing equipment.

Equipment Records

It is good operating practice to maintain records of all equipment purchased and used. This is particularly important for the critical parts of the safety system—belay ropes, seat harnesses, anchors, attachment gear, carabiners, and so forth. An efficient way to maintain equipment records and logs is to design an inventory spreadsheet that contains the name and description of each item acquired, the date that it was purchased, the cost, the manufacturer and vendor, the date of manufacture, the date the equipment was placed into service, and when it was retired. The manufacturers' recommendations for care, use, inspection, and retirement should be kept along with records indicating what the program does in each of those areas to follow the recommendations.

Summary

An important part of bringing a climbing wall to life after the wall has been constructed is to outfit the wall with all the proper equipment required to operate the wall and its climbing activities efficiently and in a cost-effective manner. What equipment to acquire and how it should be used are important considerations. The persons involved in deciding what equipment is necessary need to be knowledgeable equipment purchasers who can select and acquire proper and necessary equipment without acquiring unneeded items or items that are not approved for use with a climbing wall. Once the wall is outfitted with equipment, all supervisors, instructors, and staff involved in operating climbing wall activities need to have adequate knowledge and training on how the equipment should be used properly; how to inspect the equipment for wear and defects; when to retire equipment; and how to maintain equipment placed into service.

Developing and Managing a Climbing Program

Climbing wall operators should do everything feasible to create a climbing atmosphere that is as free of hazards and as encouraging as possible. Although indoor climbing is an inherently dangerous activity, proper education and adherence to accepted risk management and operational practices can provide a suitable margin of safety. Staff should be well prepared, and policies must be in place and followed. Climbers should understand and apply fundamental climbing skills while also adhering to established rules and protocol.

In this chapter, we present basic operating procedures, followed by general emergency preparation and practices. We also outline standards for administrators, staff, and participants, as well as the basic skills that should be mandatory for all climbing wall participants. Also included in this chapter are suggestions for selecting and configuring climbing wall holds. Strategic decisions regarding holds are necessary for heightening and sustaining interest among climbers of all abilities.

General Operating Procedures

After the wall is designed, constructed, and outfitted with equipment, the first order of business with any climbing wall, whether in a school or a public or private facility, should be the development of general operating procedures and guidelines. These will include guidelines for the facility itself, including access, rules and regulations, directions, and wall inspection. Even though you can never guarantee a completely safe climbing environment, you should always strive to reach that goal.

SAFE

SAFE may be a useful acronym to keep in mind throughout this chapter as well as when starting your day on the climbing wall.

S = Supervision. Is there adequate and appropriate supervision for the participants?

A = Ability. Is the design of the wall and are the expectations appropriate to the ability of the group?

F = Fall surface. Is it clean, free from debris, and adequate?

E = Equipment. Is it the proper equipment? Is it maintained?

Climbing Wall Manual

Before operating a climbing wall, a written manual with operations and safety procedures should be developed. Ideally, the manual should be crafted with guidance from qualified, knowledgeable climbing wall professionals. Many climbing wall manufacturers can provide useful information in this regard. Another excellent resource is the newly formed Climbing Wall Association (CWA), a nonprofit, professional industry organization for climbing wall operators. CWA was formed with the mission of providing industry risk management services and promoting industry self-regulation. The CWA is carrying on the risk management program developed by the Climbing Gym Association (CGA), a specialty group of the Outdoor Industry Association. The CWA recently obtained the rights to the "Industry Practices," the consensus-based standards developed by the CGA for the operation of climbing walls. To obtain a copy of the Industry Practices or to become a member of the CWA, visit their Web site (see appendix B for details).

A written safety procedures and operations manual provides documentation about how the wall operates and is part of the overall risk management plan. Make sure your manual is accurate and comprehensive. Key topics to include are staffing needs and responsibilities; safety protocols; policies and regulations; daily wall supervision and operating procedures; record keeping; orientations and training; and emergency action plans. Please note that this is not an all-inclusive list. Each facility will have different needs, yet some topics should be included in any manual. More extensive examples of topics, forms, and checklists may be found in appendix A.

Controlling Access to the Wall

Whether your climbing wall is in an elementary school gymnasium, a university recreation center, or a commercial climbing facility, physical access should be controlled at the facility's entrance or entrances so that unauthorized or unsupervised use does not occur. Appropriate signage and warnings should also be posted at the entrances, in addition to appropriate locations within the facility. Having a single access point is best. It should provide a place to do any paperwork, screen clientele for skill, and inform persons of the facility's rules, regulations, and requirements prior to climbing, instruction, or checkout activities. There are a number of ways this can occur. The best control of access is through a front desk or front door where all climbers check in. A separate room or location might then be used to do paperwork and screenings and to inform potential climbers before they proceed to the wall with a pass of some sort to be given to the supervising staff at the wall.

In many schools and multipurpose facilities, the climbing wall may not be in an area controlled by a secure single access point. In these situations, other means to limit unauthorized use must be instituted. For example, for a bouldering wall in an open gymnasium or hallway, you might use the gymnastics mats normally positioned underneath the wall to cover over the wall to prevent people from climbing on the wall during unsupervised periods. The mats should be secured vertically in a manner that prevents removal of the mats by unauthorized individuals, while remaining easily removable when desired.

One possible system employs wall-mounted T-nuts with bolts and hangers attached, to which the grommeted edges of the mats are secured using individual locks for each grommet or a lockable cable that is run through the mat grommets. The back sides (outsides) of the mats secured to the wall can have appropriate signage on them indicating that the wall is closed and should not be used without permission and authorized supervision. This same system could also be used for a tall wall in an open gymnasium by placing the vertical mats on the lower portion of the wall to prevent unauthorized persons from climbing on the wall. Make sure the mat coverage extends high enough from the floor to make it difficult to reach the higher exposed holds on the wall without resorting to using assistance in some form to do so.

Another system for securing a climbing wall in an otherwise open facility is to have the climbing wall surface recessed from the main wall surface somewhat so that a lockable sliding fence (similar to ones you often see securing shops in malls) can be lowered or drawn across the front of the wall to secure it.

Regardless of the method of access control, the climbing wall area must also have posted signs indicating that no climbing is allowed without proper staff supervision. Posted signs need to be prominently located in highly visible locations where entering clientele can see the signs as they approach the climbing areas, as well as in the climbing areas.

Acknowledgment and Assumption of Inherent Risks

Before participants use the climbing wall, they must be informed of the inherent risks associated with the activities in which they are to participate, and they need to accept and assume those risks in a written document before climbing. These agreements may take a variety of forms (see appendix A for several examples) and may include a request for release from liability. It is very important that climbing facility operators consult with local legal counsel to develop documents that are consistent with local and state laws.

Facility Regulations and Procedures

Regulations and procedures regarding conduct on the climbing wall typically address two areas: safety and general operating procedures. Climbing styles and wall regulations vary widely, but by establishing policies specific to a particular climbing facility, a degree of consistency at that facility may be assured. Regulations and procedures should always be posted in highly visible areas. They should be simple, clear, kept to a minimum, and, whenever possible, positively stated. In addition to rules and regulations, some facilities post directions for specific activities such as belaying instructions, climbing commands, how to tie in, and first aid procedures.

Because climbing walls differ, so do the rules and regulations that guide each wall's use. Your adopted regulations and procedures should be specific to your wall and to local and state requirements. To illustrate, while some states require signed agreements, other states require posted signage without the need for signed agreements, and yet other states require both or more.

Although facility regulations and procedures vary widely, some common categories include climber etiquette (e.g., no bouncing or swinging; respecting other climbers' space; avoiding stepping on ropes; use of chalk), climber safety (e.g., only "approved" participants may belay or climb; no free solo climbing; appropriate use of commands), and other requirements (e.g., shoes must be worn at all times; removal of jewelry before climbing; belayers must stand [no sitting]; no food or drinks permitted inside the climbing area). A more extensive list of sample regulations may be found in appendix A.

Equipping the Climber

When providing equipment to climbing wall participants, you must be organized. Ideally, an equipment sign-out sheet should be used for each person indicating the equipment being provided, its condition when signed out and returned, the time of return, and the name of the staff member who collected the returned equipment. If possible, equipment distribution and return should occur near the facility's access point.

Closing the Facility

The facility should be secured when staff are not present. There are many ways to accomplish this, depending on your situation and facility. In public schools where the climbing wall is often located in the gymnasium, securing the wall may require a different strategy than, say, at a campus recreation center where securing the climbing facility may be simply a matter of locking a single door. The ultimate goal is to secure the facility from unauthorized use, to inform people that the climbing wall facility is closed, and to make sure equipment is checked and secured properly. When securing any facility, important points to remember include inspecting all equipment prior to and following use of the wall; putting any damaged equipment aside in order to avoid its continued use (and so it can be managed at a later time); and properly displaying any "climbing wall closed" signage.

Safety Inspections

Routine safety inspections are essential for continued proper operation of the climbing facility regardless of how large or small the wall may be. Inspections should include inspection of the wall itself as well as the equipment used. The following section will provide critical safety inspection information.

Facility

Appropriate safety inspections of the wall and climbing equipment should be conducted on a regular and ongoing schedule. A log should be kept of all inspection activities. Experienced program staff generally do daily and weekly or monthly inspections. A complete structural inspection of a climbing wall should be performed periodically by a qualified licensed structural engineer familiar with climbing wall industry and local standards. Exactly when to have a structural inspection is a matter of debate. It varies greatly at this time, from the less common annually to once every five years or more. You should keep abreast of any future climbing wall industry recommendations put forth, as well as any local requirements.

Daily safety inspections should include visual inspection of the wall surface and surrounding areas. Climbing holds, belay and lead climb anchors, and quickdraws should be looked at for integrity and tightness. All equipment to be used in the day's operation—including slings, belay gear, carabiners, sit harnesses, shoes, and belay ropes—should be checked for excessive wear and improper functioning that necessitate replacement. The landing surfaces should be checked for improper function, wear, and debris. The inspections should be completed and necessary actions should be taken to remedy any problems found prior to operating the wall for the day.

Weekly or monthly safety inspections should involve a more in-depth approach looking at all aspects of the daily inspections, along with visual examination of the structure of the wall itself wherever it can be visually inspected. Physical inspections of all the belay and lead protection anchors and any attached safety gear, such as quickdraws or chains, should be done. All climbing holds on the wall should be physically and visually inspected for cracks and tightness. This should also occur anytime a new hold is placed on the wall or when a loose hold is tightened (most cracking of holds occurs while tightening them down on the wall by accidentally overtightening, which is very common and easy to do). There is no consensus on the normal scheduling of this type of inspection. Heavily used climbing walls may require a weekly schedule. Less frequently used walls may be okay with a monthly schedule. Climbing walls used as part of a class but then closed down for long periods of time need to have a more thorough safety inspection immediately prior to the start of renewed use, coupled with daily safety inspections while in use.

Sample safety inspection forms that might be adapted for daily and weekly inspections can be found in appendix A. Inspection forms need to reflect the nature of the wall being inspected. No two walls are exactly the same, so forms must be developed that are appropriate for the design, construction method, anchoring systems, and use of the wall in question.

The written results of all daily, weekly or monthly, and annual safety inspections, along with the structural inspections, should be incorporated into a manual. It is a good idea to have separate sections for each inspection category. All inspections noting problems should have a resolution page attached indicating when and how each noted problem was addressed and corrected, and who did it. A log should be maintained about who conducted an inspection, what was inspected, where and when an inspection occurred, and the findings.

Incident Reports and Damage Reports

In addition to the formal safety inspection process, climbing wall programs need to have a system in place that provides a means of communication and documentation of problems that may be observed at times other than during the inspection process. A sample equipment incident report form is provided in appendix A. Incidents often focus on unusual events that may affect the integrity of the safety system, equipment, or the wall structure itself. Common incidents that should be noted include any hard and unusual falls and all severe lead falls. All wall aspects and safety equipment involved in an incident should be identified and inspected for integrity.

Damage reports should cover any aspect of the wall or equipment that appears damaged. The reports need to be checked by all staff members when they begin their shift and by the wall manager or safety person daily, but staff members noting a problem must decide whether an immediate course of action must be taken if the problem represents an immediate safety risk. A separate manual should be used to file incident and damage reports, and each report should include a resolution page or space where details of how the report was handled or resolved is written out.

Emergency Procedures

Emergency occurrences can be greatly reduced by following industry standards for the construction, maintenance, and operation of a climbing wall, coupled with properly trained staff who competently instruct participants. However, regardless of how safe you try to make your climbing wall, accidents do happen. The best response to any accident is to be prepared. Preparedness includes developing an operations manual with emergency response procedures, ensuring that staff are properly trained, having proper first aid equipment on hand and available, and reporting all accidents and incidents.

Written Emergency Action Plan

A written plan of action for handling emergencies must be a part of the wall's safety policy and operational manual. Emergency action plans vary widely among different facilities. Nonetheless, a sample is provided in appendix A ("Rescue Belay Policy," page 160). Items included in many emergency action plans include locations and directions for exits; posted emergency phone numbers; emergency procedures in the event of an accident (sometimes also posted); accident or incident reporting policies; notification procedures; first aid and emergency equipment description and location; blood-borne pathogen protocol; rescue belay policy; and information to be released to designated agencies.

First Aid and CPR Training

Climbing wall staff should have the ability to read and interpret medical forms. Staff members need to be trained or certified in appropriate levels of first aid and CPR for their situation. A minimum of standard first aid and one-person adult CPR is commonly suggested, though many adventure programs prefer first responder levels for at least a few staff members. Most commonly, climbing walls operate in locations accessible to local EMS services, and climbing wall personnel are trained to stabilize victims for the short time needed before higher levels of help arrive to take over care. For climbing walls located in remote, less accessible locations where EMS services are over an hour away, advanced first aid training is recommended. Wilderness first aid, wilderness first responder, or EMT training might be considered in these situations.

Procedures in the Event of an Emergency

Though emergency procedures may vary from one climbing wall to another, some procedures are fairly routine and fundamental. Sample procedures for a life-threatening emergency are provided in the following example. Policies should also be in place for non-life-threatening circumstances, facility evacuation, and rescue situations. (See also "Accident and Incident Reporting" later in this section.)

LIFE-THREATENING EMERGENCY STEPS

You may be the first person to come upon and handle an emergency situation. In case of any emergency, use your first aid and CPR training. Take control of the situation, remain calm, and try to comfort the injured person as much as possible.

1. If the building manager is not in the office and there is a life-threatening emergency, do the following. If the building manager is in the office, he or she performs steps a through c while the staff member does steps 2 through 7.

   a. Call 911.

   b. Provide the following information: This is (your name). I am calling from the climbing wall at the campus recreation center. I have a life-threatening situation. Please report to the north entrance of the campus recreation center (specify location, if requested).

   c. When you call for help, you should know the following:
      - WHERE the emergency is.
      - PHONE NUMBER you are calling from (campus climbing wall: 555-1212).
      - WHAT HAPPENED.
      - NUMBER OF PERSONS needing help.
      - CONDITION OF PERSON(S): conscious or unconscious; male or female; adult or child.
      - WHAT is being done for victim.
      - BE SURE that YOU hang up last.

2. Perform emergency first aid or CPR if required. Check the ABCs (airway, breathing, circulation).

3. If another staff member is on duty, send help to get the staff member.

4. Have someone call campus police to notify them of the situation (extension 1-9999).

5. Have someone meet emergency personnel.

6. Fill out an accident report form.

7. All accident reports will be followed up by the Accident Review Committee. This committee is composed of the director of campus recreation and the faculty advisor to the climbing wall program.

Accident and Incident Reporting

All accidents where a person requires care should be investigated, recorded, and reported to the proper authorities. The purpose of this reporting is threefold: (1) to document treatment and care in case of lawsuits, (2) to comply with insurance mandates if required, and (3) to understand if certain elements or aspects of the wall are more prone to causing injuries. Incidents (near misses) should also be documented and investigated to help the program identify potential problem areas, which can then be corrected or eliminated if deemed to be a problem or source of possible future accidents.

Some groups have found the following steps to be valuable in the reporting and documenting of accidents and incidents:

- Immediately after an accident or incident has occurred, secure the scene and prevent all unauthorized entrance to the area.
- Collect all equipment, materials, or items that were involved in any way in the accident or incident.
- Complete and file an accident or incident report form immediately (no later than 24 hours after the accident).
- Have all witnesses complete witness report forms.
- Complete an equipment incident report form if climbing equipment was involved.

A sample accident or incident report form is presented in appendix A.

Accident and incident reports should normally be retained for 7 years if the participant is over 18; if the accident or incident occurs when the participant is under the age of 18, the report should be kept until 7 years after the participant reaches the age of 18. However, you should consult an attorney well versed in the laws of your state and jurisdiction about what reports and the length of time reports need to be kept.

First Aid Kits

Climbing wall programs should have one or more adequately stocked, ready-to-use first aid kits located in strategic locations in the climbing wall facility. Make sure you also meet any building or local jurisdiction requirements for locating first aid kits. Depending on the location of the wall—its distance from EMS services, facilities, and transport—the contents of a first aid kit will vary. Weekly or monthly safety inspections should include inspection of the first aid kit to make sure it is fully stocked with up-to-date supplies. A system also needs to be in place so that whenever first aid items are used, they are immediately replaced. If items that need to be restocked are not immediately available, a notice should be given to the climbing wall manager to address the inadequacy.

First aid kit contents vary considerably. A sample first aid kit contents sheet is provided in appendix A. Exact contents are based on unique qualities of each climbing wall and the staff's training, as well as any industry standards and government regulations that may apply. First aid kits must meet all state and OSHA standards that may apply to the climbing wall in question. Schools, camps, and commercial climbing wall operations may have different governing regulations that they must comply with. Other first aid items needed (besides first aid kits) may include neck collars and backboards.

Other Emergency Equipment

In some facilities, there may be ladders or even hydraulic or electric lifts located nearby. In such cases, reasonable access to that equipment must be provided, as well as training in how to move and use the equipment. For example, staff members might need to know how to position a lift, stabilize it, set up the basket, ascend safely, and then assist the climber to the ground.

Body Substance Isolation (BSI) Procedures

The climbing wall supervisor and staff should become familiar with universal precautions for the prevention of infection by blood-borne pathogens and other body substances they may come in contact with while giving first aid. They should attend appropriate training sessions on the topic. The provided first aid kits should also have appropriate BSI equipment, such as gloves, masks, one-way rescue breathing masks, glasses, disposal bags for gloves, proper cleansing agents for cleaning up contaminated wall surfaces, and so on. The program should have written protocols for the handling, packaging, cleaning, and disposal of such pathogens as well, and the staff should be trained in them.

Standards for Administrators and Staff

The following suggested standards for administrators and staff draw from a variety of sources, including the accreditation standards of the Association for Experiential Education, the standards of the Association for Challenge Course Technology, and recent "best practices" advanced by the Climbing Wall Association (CWA). Resources from these organizations are identified in appendix B.

Administrator Responsibilities

The administrator is accountable for all aspects of the climbing program and, therefore, must make concerted efforts to ensure that all program staff members possess the skills, knowledge, and experience to operate a climbing wall properly. Program staff should be able to conduct climbing activities that meet the risk management, operational, and curricular expectations of the program. Specifically, the program administrator should ensure that the following matters are being properly addressed. A file should be maintained documenting staff credentials. This file should include a set of evaluative criteria that address the ability to operate a wall that minimizes risks, and the requisite skills and knowledge to administer the program for the populations served. There should be an ongoing training and assessment program for staff that addresses competencies (see "Staff Responsibilities" later in this section) and that includes a system for keeping staff members up-to-date on changes in technology and procedures for climbing walls.

The administrator should also ensure that, whenever possible, climbs (i.e., routes and holds) are appropriate for the level of participant skills; sufficient supervision is provided (e.g., no horseplay; participants climb at an appropriate level of control and speed; warm-up exercises designed to reduce injuries and postactivity soreness are performed); and instruction is adequate and includes, but is not limited to, spotting and belaying techniques, commands/signals and communication, lowering techniques, and appropriately sequenced experiences. Staff-to-participant ratios should be appropriate for climbing wall activities. No rules apply for determining this ratio; however, to use good judgment about the number of staff assigned for climbing wall activities, the administrator must consider various safety factors, such as instructor experience and comfort level, participant age and experience level, type and difficulty of climbing activity, group size and time length, facility and equipment capacity, potential noise levels, and unique issues specific to the situation.

The administrator is responsible for making sure appropriate safety procedures are followed, such as ensuring that the following are taking place: efforts are being made to keep participants out of obvious areas of hazard from falling climbers or objects; participants are not allowed to belay until they have demonstrated competency with rope and belay systems, with harness use and tie-in, and with climbing signals; the climbing area is secured when not in use; and participants are required to wear proper clothing (e.g., remove jewelry or hats that could catch or snag on holds) and to securely fasten any protective gear.

The administrator must ensure that staff members have appropriate training in first aid, CPR, and wall rescue (e.g., proper evacuation skills). Staff should also be able to review and interpret medical forms appropriately. Adequate emergency and rescue equipment should be

It's important to ensure that climbing routes and holds are appropriate for the skill level of the climber.
© Gopher Sport

available at the site, and adequate levels of support should be available for emergency and rescue operations (see appendix A for suggested first aid kit contents).

Finally, the administrator is responsible for making sure that equipment is cared for in a suitable manner (e.g., proper storage of ropes, harnesses, carabiners, and belay devices; tightening and cleaning holds). Appropriate inspections of the wall and related equipment should be conducted prior to each use and should be documented in writing. This includes inspection of the landing surfaces (e.g., slippage, wear, properly situated). Purchase or rental, maintenance, and replacement of equipment should be properly conducted and recorded, and the administrator should determine at what point worn equipment will be replaced. Consequently, a usage and conditions log should be maintained and should follow an established schedule corresponding to inspections of the wall and associated materials. Most programs rely on outside vendors—or their own staff, if experienced—to conduct inspections that should take place on a regularly scheduled basis. The inspections will verify that holds and belay anchors are secure, and that climbing ropes and harnesses are not damaged.

Staff Responsibilities

Responsibilities for staff depend on the type of climbing and the level of supervision necessary to safeguard and guide participants. Some staff may monitor activities on a bouldering or traversing wall that involve no special climbing equipment. Other staff might not only supervise a top-roping wall (which involves specialized equipment) but also organize and present specific climbing activities intended to achieve identified goals for a specific clientele or program. Any adult staff member assigned instructional or supervisory responsibilities in a climbing wall program should possess appropriate skills based on the activities offered within that program.

Bouldering Wall Staff Requirements

The bouldering wall staff should be expected to have knowledge of and demonstrate proficiency in basic first aid and emergency procedures. They must know all safety rules and their enforcement, including rules about maximum allowable height to be climbed, spotting, horseplay, landing techniques, and use of landing zone protection.

Top-Rope Wall Staff Requirements

The top-roping wall staff should have knowledge of and demonstrate proficiency in all bouldering wall skills, plus knowledge of knots, harnesses, rappelling, anchor systems, rope and equipment care and management, rope commands, and belaying. As an additional consideration, some people predict that auto-belays and other automated "easier-to-use" systems may become the fastest growing segment of the climbing industry, yet perhaps also the most problematic. For example, as new devices appear on the market, each may have distinctive details. In some cases, such devices may be used in ways contrary to the manufacturer's intended use. For that reason, top-rope wall staff may need to become familiar with specifics of these systems as well.

Specifics for Belaying

First, a cautionary note: When checking an individual's competencies in belaying (and, for that matter, spotting), the check or test is merely a snapshot in time. In other words, a competency check provides only a summary of a person's skills at a particular time. It does not ensure that thc skills will appear later and with the same attentiveness as demonstrated during the check. This matter cannot be overstated and will be emphasized at other times in this book. With that caveat in mind, more detailed belaying expectations include satisfactory demonstration of the following:

- Correctly tie the following knots:
  - Figure eight follow-through knot (this is a standard tie-in knot for the climber; although some programs may use a bowline knot, the figure eight follow-through is more intuitive and easier to inspect)
  - Double fisherman's knot (typically used as a safety or backup knot to secure the tie-in knot; also can be used to join two ends of accessory cord to form a sling)
- Correctly fit and tie into a harness (many harnesses require some special buckling procedure or a specific way to tie in or double tie in points; if these procedures are neglected, the harness is rendered potentially dangerous). Always adhere to the manufacturer's instructions.
- Use proper belay procedures, including correct use of the following:
  - All belay devices approved for the program's climbing wall (the spectrum of available belay devices continues to increase, including Sticht plate, Lowe Tuber, Trango Pyramid and Jaws, Black Diamond ATC, Wild Country Variable Controller, and Metolius BRD, as well as belay devices possessing an integral cam-type system such as the Petzl Grigri, among others)
  - An effective body belay

Ultimately, it is the climbing wall administrator's responsibility to monitor and enforce the application of the above skills and safety procedures by adult staff members.

Standards for Participants

This section contains recommended standards that climbing wall programs may apply to any participant who wants to use a bouldering wall or a top-rope wall. Some general, basic requirements are provided, followed by a more detailed list of specific expectations.

Bouldering Requirements

Participants in bouldering must demonstrate compliance with climbing wall rules; basic understanding of the facility and program components; and competence in landing techniques, spotting techniques, and the use of landing zone surfaces. In most cases, the climbing wall should not be used in any fashion without the presence of designated staff to supervise the activities. Some programs may permit unsupervised bouldering, and they typically delineate the process and circumstances that allow this to occur. You should also note that supervisors cannot be expected to be in all places at all times. Hence, every boulderer needs to use good judgment, and programs should consider our recommendation (see below) to use adequate spotting.

Before using the climbing wall, participants should have completed appropriate contracts and agreements such as waivers, indemnification agreements, consent forms, and rules (for examples, see appendix A). These forms should be on file or presented at the time of climbing.

We recommend that you consider using spotters. All spotters should be taught and should be required to demonstrate appropriate spotting techniques. Furthermore, participants should not walk or stand underneath a boulderer while she is on the wall, nor boulder beneath a climber or another boulderer. Boulderers should be prohibited from climbing above a designated line. At some walls, a boulderer's feet are not permitted above a horizontal three-foot (91-centimeter) line, or the boulderer's hands are not permitted above a horizontal eight-foot (243-centimeter) line. More frequently, the requirement is that a boulderer's feet may not exceed his or her shoulder height. Safety requirements should be appropriate to the users. For instance, the range of sizes and abilities of boulderers who use a college bouldering wall may differ from those using a community center's wall or a wall in an elementary school. Furthermore, if a bouldering wall has overhangs, this directive should be adjusted according to the nature of the overhang (height, angle, types and placement of holds). And finally, landing surfaces should be adequate for the bouldering wall and its intended users.

Top-Roping Requirements

Participants in top-roping must fulfill all previously stated bouldering requirements (except belayers replace spotters, and climbers may climb above the bouldering line), plus demonstrate knowledge of double-check (belayer and climber double-check each element in their safety system—both participants double-check themselves, then each other); belaying; harnesses; knots; rappelling (optional program component); rope and equipment care and management; and climbing commands. In the following sections, specific expectations for climbers and belayers are provided (preceded by some general climbing stipulations). All safety guidelines should be written with climbers' and belayers' safety in mind. By taking time to follow prescribed guidelines, participants help to ensure continuation of a program.

General Stipulations

1. The climbing wall should not be used in any fashion without the presence of designated climbing wall staff.

2. Before using the climbing wall, participants should have completed appropriate contracts and agreements. These forms must be on file or presented at the time of climbing.

3. Although the staff conducts regular safety inspections of climbing walls and equipment, each participant is responsible for informing climbing wall staff of possible safety hazards.

4. Before each climb, partners must use the buddy system to double-check harness buckles, knots, and belay devices. In the event of a disagreement, participants should ask a climbing wall staff member to perform the final safety check.

5. Behavior not in accord with climbing wall policies may result in immediate dismissal from the climbing wall and loss of climbing privileges.

Climber Requirements

1. Tie directly into the harness using a figure eight follow-through knot with an acceptable backup knot.

2. Remove any jewelry such as long necklaces, dangling earrings, and bracelets that might get caught on holds.

3. Wear loose fitting, comfortable clothing that will allow for ease of movement and adequate ventilation. Care should be taken to pull back or put up long hair.

4. Use only climbing shoes or athletic footwear. The added cost of close-fitting climbing shoes with sticky rubber base soles is worthwhile. These shoes are lightweight, sensitive when placing feet on holds, and permit the climber to "stick" to the wall. Hard rubber base, higher heel, or cleated bottom shoes are not well suited to indoor climbing and may make unsightly marks on a wall. For any shoes borrowed from the program, a staff member should spray those shoes with disinfectant after each use. Although a few climbers may prefer to climb with bare feet or flip-flop sandals, health code issues usually prevent it. And a "no barefoot climbing" policy is consoling to those of us who don't enjoy placing our hands and fingers on other climbers' toe jam!

5. Use chalk balls only instead of loose chalk. Loose chalk can contribute to a dusty climbing environment. Although some programs do not permit any form of chalk, a reasonable compromise (many climbers are fond of chalk for drying clammy fingers) is to allow

chalk balls. Chalk may be deposited on the wall and holds, but it is much less airborne with the use of a chalk ball.

6. Be alert to indoor climbing hazards such as falling or swinging climbers, a crux set too low (see "Setting Routes" later in this chapter), objects on the floor, and so on.

7. Avoid overuse injuries (i.e., monitor fatigue, use proper technique, and know your limits!).

8. Do not climb above anchors, touch anchors, grasp the top of the climbing wall, or interfere with lighting, pipes, or other fixtures. Staff in charge of facilities should check for sharp objects and edges at tops and sides of the wall.

9. After completing a climb, ask to down climb or to be lowered with legs apart and feet against the wall. Bouncing on the way down is not acceptable because it increases the need for belayer attention, can tug the belayer off balance causing him to release his grip on the brake, and can cause the climber to turn sideways and hit his head on a hold or the wall. Slow, controlled descents are preferable to mimicking "be all that you can be" military advertisements that showcase rappelling from a helicopter or down a steep cliff.

10. Bouldering must occur below designated heights and may not interfere with top-roped climbers or belayers.

Belayer Requirements

1. Only participants who have completed a safety process (e.g., passed a belay check, a safety orientation, or whatever your gym requires) conducted by climbing wall staff may climb, use the wall, or belay. Since lead climbing involves some different techniques and requirements, a separate training or check is required. The same applies if using a different type of belay device (e.g., one with automatic features). In other words, a single orientation may not be appropriate in settings that involve an array of climbing and belaying options.

2. Belay checks will be administered only to participants who have completed appropriate belay instruction that has either been conducted by or approved by climbing wall staff, or who can demonstrate sufficient previous climbing experience.

3. To qualify for a belay check, the participant must demonstrate the following:
   • Understanding of customary climbing wall rules as well as any that may be unique to the facility.
   • How to properly fit an approved harness.
   • How to tie directly into the harness according to the manufacturer's recommended tie-in location using a figure eight follow-through knot (with an acceptable backup knot, if required).

- How to give and respond to appropriate belay commands.
- Careful, acceptable belaying skills, including
  - use of approved locking carabiner and belay device;
  - taking up rope (slack);
  - catching unexpected falls;
  - lowering a climber slowly;
  - assuming an "athletic stance" and proper positioning while belaying (sitting or kneeling is not allowed while belaying); and
  - fastidious implementation of the double-check!

4. A belayer must tuck in or control in some fashion any loose clothing or hair that could become entangled in belay devices.

5. A belayer must focus attention on the climber at all times. Belays should have no slack.

6. A belayer must make sure that no one stands beneath a climber in such a way that, in the event of a fall, there may be potential for injury to the climber or to others.

7. Backup belayers should be used in some circumstances (e.g., for beginning belayers and youngsters who may be more comfortable with added security; or when the climber weighs significantly more than the belayer).

Climbing Wall Skills

Throughout this book, we emphasize the importance of creating a climbing setting that is reassuring and encouraging. Certainly, when potential hazards are reduced and sound protocol is established and followed, the quality of a climbing site is enhanced. However, when participants acquire and practice fundamental climbing skills (e.g., body position, spotting and belaying, equipment use, knots, and communication), the margin of safety increases, thereby offering a more secure, fun experience for everyone. All participants should understand and apply fundamental climbing skills.

Spotting

Even though climbers should climb no higher than a specified line (e.g., you may specify that a climber's feet may not exceed her shoulder height), the potential for injury from a fall is stubbornly present. Thus, all bouldering or traversing activity requires a spotter who actively safeguards the movements of the climber. In addition, spotting is also a part of lead climbing. A lead climber should receive spotting until clipped into the first protection anchor. The responsibilities of spotting, especially specific techniques for any individual overhangs, should be taught and practiced. Spotters must be comfortable with their knowledge of spotting and with the requirements and skills of their role.

Falls can be harmful to both the faller and spotter alike. The primary duty of spotters is to support and protect the head and upper body of a climber in case a fall should occur. Secondary duties usually involve guarding against a participant's uncontrolled, fast movements that also could result in injury (e.g., a twisted ankle, sprained wrist, or dislocated knee). Instruct spotters to focus continuously on the climber. A spotter's knees should be flexed slightly to absorb impact, with one foot slightly in front of the other, and arms and hands extended toward the climber. Teach spotters to position themselves in anticipation of a possible fall, yet not to make physical contact unless a fall occurs. The object is for the falling climber to fall against the spotters' hands. Spotters, therefore, cushion a fall rather than catch a fall. Although poor spotting is unsafe and can have detrimental effects on a climber, good spotting results in increased individual confidence and a greater sense of trust among group members. It also leads to everyone becoming more safety conscious and responsible for one another.

Spotting for bouldering should be accompanied by specific commands so that a climber does not climb before spotters are ready. Typical commands are as follows:

> *Climber: "Ready?"*
>
> *Spotter: "Ready."*
>
> *Climber: "Climbing."*
>
> *Spotter: "Climb."*

The role of a climbing wall staff member is to ensure that spotters are (1) competent and comfortable with their responsibilities, (2) placed appropriately (e.g., spotters should spot other appropriately sized participants), and (3) sufficient in number to prevent injury should someone fall. Generally one or two spotters can actively look after a single climber. Concerns about spotting may be a greater issue in a community recreation center (where a 10-year-old girl is belaying her 200-pound dad) than in a college facility where age and size differences may not be as likely. The staff member should also assure that climbers are not allowed to climb too high and that the landing area is level and free of obstacles.

Knot Tying

Knots are primarily used to connect climbers to the rope. In addition to a primary knot, knots are also used as a backup in order to secure primary tie-in knots. Moreover, by allowing a person to temporarily attach one thing to another, knots can be used to attach ropes and webbing together as well as to create slings for carrying gear. There are many specific knots for many specific situations. Listed in appendix B are several excellent books that pictorially display various knots and tying sequences.

The following are a few fundamental knots for use on climbing walls. You can always learn more, but these should suffice in most climbing wall situations.

Figure Eight Follow-Through

The figure eight follow-through is the standard tie-in knot (figure 5.1). A few climbers still prefer the bowline, which for decades was the accepted way to tie in. However, use of the bowline as a tie-in has generally fallen out of favor, being replaced with a figure eight follow-through knot. Also known as a trace figure eight, the figure eight follow-through is secure, easy to tie and to inspect, and simple to teach. In addition, once tied, the figure eight can remain in the rope so that subsequent climbers need only trace or follow it rather than completely tying a new knot (this is not possible with the bowline). The figure eight follow-through should be knotted correctly or "dressed," which means that there are no extraneous twists ("a not neat knot need not be knotted") and, for security, the knot has been cinched tightly by pulling on each strand. All knots should be dressed because, although only marginally stronger than undressed ones, they are easier to check and to untie once loaded.

Double Fisherman's Knot

The double fisherman's knot is used to back up the primary tie-in knot (figure 5.2). When cinched tightly, it stays tight. It should be cinched snugly against the primary tie-in knot leaving about three inches (7.6 centimeters) of tail. Although a properly tied figure eight follow-through with adequate tail (as a general rule, twice as long as the knot itself) doesn't require a double fisherman's backup, many instructors choose to add a safety knot

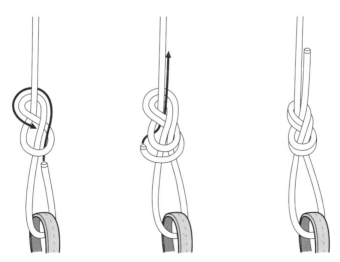

FIGURE 5.1   Follow-through knot.

anyway. The double fisherman's knot can also be used to tie a length of standard six- or seven-millimeter accessory cord into a sling.

Water Knot

The water knot or ring bend is the classic knot used to tie two pieces or two ends of webbing together (figure 5.3). Since nylon webbing is slippery,

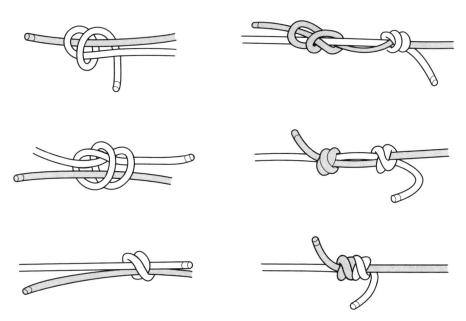

FIGURE 5.2 Double fisherman's knot.

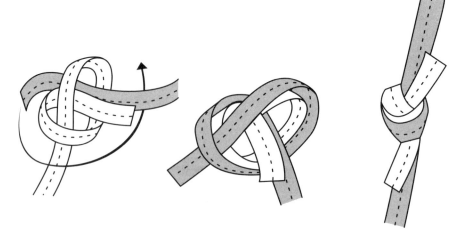

FIGURE 5.3 Water knot.

the water knot has a tendency to become untied. Thus, the tails must extend at least three inches (7.6 centimeters)—some say a fist width—and the knot should be inspected before each use.

Belaying

Since belaying is a technique that protects the climber in case of a fall, good belaying is one of the most important fundamentals in a climbing program. A rope is attached to the climber, and the rope then runs to an anchor and to the belayer. Stationed on the ground, the belayer manages the rope in order to catch or lower the climber in a cautious, controlled manner.

The climbing rope runs from the anchor through a belay device that is attached to the belayer's harness by means of a locking carabiner. When the rope is bent across it, the belay device provides friction, or stopping power. The rope passes into the belay device, around the carabiner, and out through the belay device again. Use of a belay device requires very little strength to hold a fall and, when properly rigged and operated, provides considerable security to the whole system.

In the actual process of belaying, the belayer uses a guide hand and a brake hand, which never leaves the rope. The guide hand (on the side of the rope going to the climber) pulls in slack as the climber ascends. The brake hand (on the side of the rope after it has passed through the belay device) also pulls in slack and is ready to quickly apply friction in order to check a fall. Thus the guide hand pulls rope toward the belay device, and the brake hand pulls rope away, keeping the rope snug. Not only should the belayer keep the brake hand on the rope at all times, but he should also keep the brake itself on at all times, except when paying out and taking in rope. Inattentive belayers frequently violate the latter requirement, thereby compromising the system's effectiveness.

Several methods of belaying are effective. For example, the "slip, slap, slide" method is easy to demonstrate and is well suited to the hip belay, but it does not work well with modern belay devices and presents the possibility of pinching or grasping both rope strands (the guide section going to the climber and the braking section) while belaying. The BUS (Brake, guide hand Under brake hand, Slide) method works well with modern belay devices and leaves the brake hand in the braking position longer than does the "slip, slap, slide" method, but the BUS method can only take in a small amount of rope at a time. Presented here is a method that is suited to modern friction devices, is easy to learn, and minimizes improper pinching. Referred to as the discrete hand switch, some prefer this method because it also permits taking in more rope at a time than does the BUS method. Finally, although not permitting the brake hand to remain in the braking position quite as long as in the BUS method, the time differential is minimal once this method is learned.

1. Start with both hands in the ready position: The guide hand grasps the rope approximately 12 to 18 inches (30 to 45 centimeters) above the belay device, while the brake hand holds the rope bent across the device.
2. With the guide hand, pull the rope through the belay device while simultaneously extending the brake hand.
3. Release the guide hand (not the brake hand—the brake hand never leaves the rope!) and grasp the rope above the brake hand (which continues to hold the rope firmly).
4. Slide the brake hand back toward the belay device and apply the brake, returning the guide hand to the starting position.

This technique is relatively easy for belayers to learn. Also, if a climber should fall while the brake hand is sliding, the brake hand is ready to quickly assume the braking position. A key principle is "the brake is always on unless paying out or taking in rope." Too frequently, a belayer's brake hand is holding onto the rope, but the brake is not being applied. Keep in mind that belaying is an essential skill that should be taught by a professional and practiced regularly by belayers. *The information in this book is intended to be used in addition to, not in place of, training from professionals.*

A few additional comments about belaying should be considered. Although good belaying requires proper application of friction, the ability to stop a falling climber depends on several things. First, a belayer's attention must remain focused on the climber at all times. After all, the climber is entrusting her well-being to the belayer. Second, the belayer should be properly braced, anticipating the impact of force and the direction of pull caused by the falling climber. Belayers should keep one leg forward at all times. Third, in cases of a sizeable weight difference between the climber and belayer, or perhaps when an individual has not belayed for a while and calls for added security, a fixed anchor or backup belayer should be considered for extra protection from a fall.

Communicating

Effective communication facilitates an exchange of information between climber and belayer and, thus, is essential for safety. In addition to eye contact, the belayer should maintain voice contact with the climber at all times (if distance and noise level permit). A standard protocol of communication removes any doubt about what the climber and belayer are doing. One system, developed by Paul Petzoldt (Powers 1993), uses commands that are usable and understandable in all conditions. Thus, they easily transfer to outdoor rock-climbing situations where loud wind, the roar of a river, or long distances between climber and belayer may result in words being misunderstood. This system of communication begins with the belayer and combines number of syllables with cadence.

SYSTEMS OF COMMUNICATION FOR CLIMBING

Belayer: when ready says, "On, belay" (three syllables)

Climber: when ready to climb says, "Climbing" (two syllables)

Belayer: tells climber to go on by saying, "Climb" (one syllable)

Since noise may be less of a factor at an indoor climbing wall, and since some programs prefer to initiate commands with the climber, another system of communication is as follows:

Climber: when clipped in says, "Am I safe, Terry?" or "On belay?"

Belayer: when ready says, "You're safe, Luis" or "Belay is on"

Climber: when ready to climb says, "Climbing"

Belayer: tells climber to go on by saying, "Climb"

Regardless of the system adopted in your program, you should ensure that commands are understood, used, and mastered by all participants. Both parties should agree that the climber may not begin climbing until the belayer has given permission. Here are some additional commands to consider:

Climber: if rope is too tight, says, "Slack"

Belayer: responds with around six inches (15 centimeters) of slack rope to each command, saying, "Thank you" (optional, but a nice, generic acknowledgment that the last command was heard)

Climber: if rope is too loose, says, "Up rope"

Belayer: takes available slack out of rope, saying, "Thank you"

Climber: at the top of the climb, says, "Take" or "Tension"

Belayer: takes up slack and assures brake is on, saying, "Thank you"

Climber: to indicate she wishes to be lowered back to the ground, says, "Lower me" (sometimes preceded by "Got me?")

Belayer: lowers climber slowly, saying, "I've got you" or "Thank you"

Climber: when off belay, says, "Belay off" (different cadence from "On belay")

Belayer: only then removes brake hand, saying, "Thank you"

Sometimes when climbers anticipate or are worried about an impending fall, they shout, "Falling!" or "Watch me!" Since the belayer should be continuously applying the brake (except when paying out or taking in rope), the response should be "Thank you" or "I've got you."

Setting Routes

A climber's experience will not depend only on his or her climbing skills—just as important is the layout of the climbing wall. By varying the difficulty of climbing holds and routes, a wide range of climbers can be served on a single wall. If holds are too small, or too far apart, or inappropriately positioned, many climbers will not experience the success and enjoyment that is possible on a well-balanced wall. Thus, this section provides advice about the placement of holds (setting routes). A discussion of the holds themselves may be found in chapter 2.

Just as there are no typical holds, there is no such thing as a typical route. Since every wall varies according to the designer and the available materials, climbing routes should suit the shape and size of a particular wall and the needs and abilities of the climbers. Fortunately, most walls have removable holds that can be repositioned to create a potentially limitless variety of climbing routes. Walls that do not permit repositioning should be avoided since they may present a configuration that does not support a program's needs, and that configuration cannot be amended. The configuration of holds is crucial to the success of your program. Routes that are too demanding may discourage even a top-notch climber. Likewise, a route that is too monotonous or effortless will quickly lose its appeal. The key is to design routes that present sufficient challenges to everyone.

In addition to providing consultation in wall design and construction, some companies will assist you in designing your routes. Eventually the routes will need to be reconfigured for variety or to better suit client needs and interests. At that point, most routes are set by climbing wall staff who want to ensure that clients—experienced and newcomers alike—will feel secure and appropriately challenged.

When developing routes, consultation with climbing wall companies and experienced climbers can provide valuable assistance. Furthermore, due to safety issues related to route setting, proper training is also important. In earlier chapters, when discussing the design and construction of climbing walls, we touched on the installation of holds. However, some of that discussion bears directly on route development and thus warrants attention here. The following guidelines should provide a good start for novices as they configure or reconfigure a wall. Most walls provide a random pattern for installing holds, and T-nut and hold "density" should be considered. It is neither necessary nor recommended to place a hold in every available space on the wall (i.e., in every existing T-nut location). By the same token, large spaces between holds should be avoided. In addition, walls used by children in a school or community center may require closer spacing of holds than walls in a college recreation center (e.g., 12 versus 10 holds and 60 versus 50 T-nuts per four-by-eight-foot [121-by-243-centimeter] panel); and a traversing wall usually contains more T-nuts (normally 80 to 100, yet up to 150 holds per panel) than a tall climbing wall does. Keeping these considerations in mind, a typical distance between holds may be 1 or 2 feet (30 or 60 centimeters), and a nice range of holds is 10 holds per 32 square feet (2.9 square meters). The number of holds will also depend, of course, on availability and cost.

When creating routes for your program, consider these steps:

1. Install holds in the bottom few rows. These require footholds that stand out from the wall and provide a solid surface that is easy to stand on. If the wall is designed exclusively for bouldering or traversing, the bottom row will require more holds than the next couple of rows will. Holds in those rows may be two to four feet (60 to 121 centimeters) apart and should be placed under the high points of traverses.

2. Install holds in remaining rows using two general principles. First, put holds in locations obvious to the climber; that is, where the climber's hand will be on the top of the hold, pulling down and in. For bouldering walls, install enough of these for a climber to completely traverse the wall. Second, install additional holds that may not be as obvious to the climber. These holds should be placed in various directions requiring the climber to pull up on the bottom of the hold while pushing down with the feet (undercling) or to lean away from the hold and pull from the side (sidepull) in order to stay on the wall.

3. After installing all of the holds, ask several participants to attempt traverses or vertical climbs looking for trouble spots (e.g., holds too far apart, not enough straightforward holds, not enough tricky holds, too many easy holds). These participants should reflect your entire clientele. For example, stronger climbers may be comfortable using a smaller hold on a more overhanging wall. When spicing things up and adding some challenge for these climbers, take care not to overlook the needs of less-capable climbers. In other words, set routes that will "please the crowds."

4. Mix routes of various difficulties; in other words, evenly distribute route difficulties throughout the facility. When feasible, include a variety of challenges in a single route.

5. If you name your routes, make sure the names are appropriate. If you tab your routes, post useful information about the routes (e.g., holds marked in red or as double black diamonds present a high degree of difficulty).

Routes should not only be routinely reset, but should also be checked for safety. A common mistake is to overtighten holds causing them to break. This is especially true in instances of irregular concrete surfaces behind some holds. Be careful! Also, the best time for washing chalk and grime off holds is when a route is changed. Products such as Simple Green are easy to use and biodegradable. Holds can also be soaked in muriatic acid; but, since it is an acid, care must be taken (e.g., wear acid-resistant gloves, use baking soda for spills, and carefully follow the manufacturer's instructions). Dishwashers are great assets for cleaning most holds because they are fast and easy, and they minimize the work involved in cleaning large numbers of holds at one time. Finally, since route setting can be time consuming, supervisors should be sure to allocate enough time to complete all route-setting tasks (including cleanup time) to keep operations running smoothly.

Summary

Your staff is well prepared, written policies and operating procedures are in place, and participants are ready to apply fundamental climbing skills and to adhere to established rules and protocol. In other words, everyone is raring to go! In the next chapter, we will present activities for enhancing climbing wall experiences, and strategies for inventing your own activities.

Climbing Activities and Games

This chapter is designed for anyone who wants to provide climbing wall experiences and challenges appropriate to a wide range of interests and abilities. We will present specific games and activities as well as strategies that you can use to discover and invent your own endless variations. As mentioned in previous chapters, climbing walls have many uses: instructional purposes, recreation, fitness and training, and competition. Depending on a program's aims, instructors sometimes take on different roles. For example, one instructor may teach basic climbing skills to children; another may offer problem-solving opportunities to corporate groups; while yet another may oversee a year-round training program. Activities and services should be consistent with a program's stated mission or published literature.

No single book can adequately address all of the intricacies of being a climbing wall teacher, facilitator, or trainer. Therefore, sources for more information on planning games and activities are listed in appendix B. Also, this chapter does not focus on instruction per se, nor do we pretend to offer a movement-based curriculum. Rather, we present "wall-tested" activities that you can use to further your instructional efforts. We also present some strategies for modifying activities and for creating your own activities. Before proceeding to activities, however, it may be useful to highlight some basic climbing skills and concepts. In the previous chapter, we discussed safety considerations (e.g., knots and communication). In this chapter, we begin with movement—the fun stuff, the essence of the activity.

Basic Movement Skills

Climbing involves power and endurance, is remarkably cardiovascular, and necessitates moving from one balance position to another, all the while attempting to conserve energy. The basic principles when moving are simple: Regular breathing keeps muscles oxygenated and ready to function; large muscles can do more work than smaller muscles; and bones do not tire. Since legs are stronger than arms, and since the skeleton does not tire, climbing success depends heavily on balancing over your feet. Keeping your body weight on your feet is critical to success, and the key to movement is smooth transfer of your weight from foot to foot.

Footwork

Footwork is what matters most. Look at various options and choose moves that maintain balance over one or two feet. Small steps permit more balanced weight transfers, and flexibility affords more options. Edging refers to the use of the inside (your strongest and generally most effective) or outside edge of the foot to stand on small flat holds (figure

6.1). If a hold is less well defined (e.g., a sloping hold that does not permit edging), then smearing may be a more appropriate technique. Smearing involves applying weight by rubbing the sole of your shoe on the hold to gain friction. Realize that most of the time you are not just edging or smearing, but doing some of both. Although other techniques such as toe cams and heel hooks can be useful, much success can be found by refining your basic edging and smearing skills.

Good habits are hard to break. So be deliberate in looking for and choosing footholds. The security of a foothold depends largely on how much weight you can put on it. Edging involves balancing your weight directly over an edge, while smearing involves putting weight directly over your shoe to create friction between your shoe and the hold. For both edging and smearing, your body position over your feet is critical to remaining on the hold.

FIGURE 6.1   Edging.

Hands

In chapter 2, we described some types of holds that a climber might encounter (e.g., jugs, edges, pinches, and pockets). Climbers use their hands to assist in balancing over their feet, or to hold themselves in place while moving from one location or position to another. Remember, your arms and hands are not as strong as your legs; to the greatest extent possible, your hands should be used mainly as balance points.

Most holds are placed in such a manner that there are a variety of ways to use them. In order to hold onto the wall, your hand is frequently on top of a hold, pulling down and in. Using holds in this fashion is usually quite obvious, although different holds may require different techniques. A tiny edge may be just big enough to be held with the first digit of four or fewer fingers, while a large jug with a gripping surface that is tilted in toward the wall may provide excellent grip or "purchase." Similarly, pockets permit inserting fingers into a hole, while pinches require grasping

FIGURE 6.2   Climber using counterpressure.

the hold between the thumb and fingertips. Regardless of the type of hold and grip, whenever you can release from a hold, let that hand relax for a moment. Keeping your arms and hands in a flexed position will cause them to tire more quickly than if you rest them for short periods.

Additional Techniques

Some holds permit less obvious ways of using them and require the use of counterpressure, which involves pushing or pulling in opposite directions (figure 6.2). In an undercling, for example, to stay on the wall you pull up on the bottom of the hold, while pushing with your feet. Another example of counterpressure is a sidepull or lie-back, which means gripping the hold from the side and leaning with your entire body away from the hold. This technique permits you to put considerable weight onto your feet, allowing greater purchase on some footholds. Another useful counterpressure strategy is stemming, which involves pushing outward with both feet at the same time. Since equal weight is placed on both feet, counterpressure must be provided with a hand in order to move a foot. A good use for stemming is resting, especially in inside corners. Finally, an extreme example of counterpressure is flagging, where a reach in one direction is countered by dangling one leg in the opposite direction. This technique allows you to balance your weight over a foothold while leaning out and grabbing a distant handhold.

Resting

As we mentioned earlier, climbing can be tiring and thus requires energy conservation. Since muscles tire, resting on your skeleton is an important means of conserving energy. Several resting tips can help in extending your climbing time and efficiency. First, stand tall on straight legs, and hang down on straight arms. Lowering your heels will relax the calves, and straightening your elbow will relax the biceps.

Second, if you must rely on muscles, use them in the most effective position. Intermediate positions such as a partially bent arm or leg are usually the weakest, so full contraction or full extension is more desirable. Use larger muscles whenever you can. Likewise, rest smaller muscles frequently. Searching for resting spots is very important, as is moving quickly from one resting spot to another.

Third, devise a workable strategy. One of the world's greatest climbers, Lynn Hill, is said to possess an uncanny ability to plan her moves in advance from the ground. Thus, visual inspection may be useful for deciphering a route and planning moves in advance. Asking others for their opinions about your intended route may also be helpful.

Strategies for Designing Activities

Before proceeding to some already designed activities, you should become familiar with the following strategies drawn from concepts in *Changing Kids' Games* (Morris and Stiehl 1999). These simple strategies are useful for devising or modifying any climbing activity in order to suit every participant's needs, interests, and abilities. With proper motivation and ingenuity, any instructor can develop climbing wall activities appropriate to all participants and goals.

CHANGE, CHALLENGE, AND CHOICE

Step One

Change. Whether adopting or adapting an activity, some changes are usually necessary—or at least useful. For example, suppose two climbers are involved in a game where, starting from opposite ends on a wall, each tries to retrieve a single bandanna placed in the center of the wall. The routes to the bandanna have not been altered in quite some time, leading to boredom. Simply changing the routes can revive the climbers' interest in this game. Besides routes, other aspects to change might include the following:

- Holds: size, texture, direction, number, pattern, distance from each other
- Equipment or materials: bandannas, hoops, tape (for marking routes), chalk, shoe boxes, marking pens, beanbags, cowbell, ball of yarn or string
- Players: individuals, pairs, teams
- Movements: hand over hand; underclings; sidepulls; long and short reaches; outside edge of foot

(continued)

- Rules: touch only orange holds; use all holds in the route; use only eight total holds; complete route in less than two minutes; pass through vertical hoop; retrieve ball and place in shoe box placed at start of route; traverse while blindfolded

Later in the chapter, it should become obvious that, with a little ingenuity, you can convert virtually any board game, card game, and indoor or outdoor game into a climbing wall activity. For instance, Cooperative Climbs derives from relay races, Spell a Word is an adaptation of Scrabble, and Ghost draws from a family pastime on long car trips.

Step Two

Challenge. Sometimes an activity should be changed to reduce boredom, as in the case of the above game where the routes had become familiar and stagnant. But another more common reason for change is to adjust the challenge. Again using the bandanna game, suppose one climber is significantly stronger and more skilled than the other. Competition is most satisfying and enjoyable between two players of relatively equal ability. In this scenario, the more capable climber may become bored, and the less capable climber might become unduly frustrated. These circumstances can be overcome by changing the degree of difficulty for one or both climbers. For example, to increase the degree of difficulty for the more capable climber, extend the distance to be traversed, intensify the route by reducing the size or number of usable holds, or require that she transport some object during the climb. Comparable changes that reduce the level of difficulty might encourage the less advanced climber. By changing an activity in order to deliberately adjust its challenge, an instructor can assure that the task will be neither too difficult nor too easy for a given individual or group.

Step Three

Choice. "Always offer choices. A coerced player is no longer a player" (Rohnke and Grout 1998, p. 15). Even though a climbing activity might be changed with the intent to alter its degree of difficulty, usually no single change will accommodate everyone. But if climbers have an opportunity to choose among several options, the invitation to participate, to try, and to risk is enhanced. Again using the bandanna game, a simple and subtle change might have significant consequences. The more advanced climber may select one of the following options: a longer route of moderate difficulty; a shorter but more challenging route; the requirement that she must retrieve two bandannas placed some distance apart. By choosing among several options, climbers select their own level of challenge.

Practice and Game Activities

These activities are designed to help climbers develop and diversify their climbing skills. Each activity is presented in the following format: name of the activity, equipment required, description, safety considerations, and variations. Some activities are specifically designated for bouldering or traversing and some may be used for either. When supervising these activities, instructors should adhere to the general safety precautions outlined in the previous chapter. Any additional safety considerations specific to the following activities are noted in the description of that activity.

MIRRORING

Equipment
None

Description
In pairs, climbers choose a leader and follower (mirror). As the leader traverses the wall, the follower attempts to copy the leader's movements (figure 6.3). Roles may be switched according to instructor directions (e.g., after completing a traverse; after a predetermined number of attempts; determined by each pair).

Safety Considerations
Followers should be responsible for maintaining an arm's-length distance between themselves and their leader. Each pair should be at least four arm's lengths from the next pair. Remaining pairs can serve as spotters.

Variations
- Specific moves are required (e.g., cross hands or feet at least once; attempt at least one undercling).
- Event is timed (e.g., pairs estimate how long their traverse will take).
- Second leader must attempt to replicate the first leader's entire route and moves.

FIGURE 6.3 Mirroring.

SPELL A WORD

Equipment

Small pieces of masking tape with a letter of the alphabet on each

Description

Before the session, the instructor attaches letters of the alphabet underneath climb-ing holds, and also places into a box words that can be formed from the letters. Climbers participate in pairs or small groups. One climber selects a word from the box. With support from partners, the climber must touch every hold representing a letter in that word (figure 6.4).

FIGURE 6.4   Spell a Word.

Safety Considerations

Partners should be reminded to assist climbers in locating letters, but not at the expense of performing their duties as a spotter or belayer. Letters should be placed so that several climbers can climb without interfering with one another.

Variations

- Letters must be touched in sequence.
- Several holds may contain more than one letter.
- If a letter appears more than once in a word (e.g., *s* in scissors), that letter must be touched only once.
- Climbers may select from among several visible words (hence a choice) or may simply reach into the box and select a word by chance. Another option might be to choose between a visible word and a luck-of-the-draw word.
- Climbers spell their own name, or a word that relates to a theme (e.g., summer fun, nutritious foods, forms of exercise, pets).
- Rather than letters, words are placed on each piece of masking tape. Climbers must travel from word to word creating a sentence. Subsequent climbers may not use the same sentence.
- Again using words, climbers must traverse to the Spanish equivalents of several English words selected from the box.
- Provide math problems by replacing letters with numbers (e.g., 1 to 5). Climbers now must select a number from the box (e.g., 64) and then touch holds to reach that sum. Increase the challenge by placing higher numbers farther away (thereby increasing climbing time).
- Same as previous variation, but climber must subtract numbers from the selected number (e.g., 64) until reaching zero.

CLIMB FOR TIME

Equipment

Individual progress cards (include climber's name, date, time on wall)

Description

Individual climbers attempt to increase their climbing time, thereby increasing their muscular and cardiovascular endurance. Climbers can gauge personal improvement by charting their "climb time" progress (i.e., time they remain on the wall bouldering and top-roping).

Safety Considerations

Climbers should be encouraged to challenge themselves but to remain on the wall only as long as they feel secure and in control of their bodies. Instructors and spotters or belayers should monitor each climber's level of fatigue and inform him that it is okay to stop and to try again later. Also, instructors should stress that this is not a group competition. Rather, it is each climber's responsibility to strive for personal bests.

Variations

- Climbers estimate how long they will remain (or did remain) climbing.
- Climbers set goal times (e.g., 4 minutes), and then stop after reaching that goal.
- Certain routes or holds must be attempted, or avoided.
- Climbers must attempt to increase their previous best by a prescribed time only (e.g., no more than 30 seconds).
- In addition to estimating length of time, climbers also estimate number of holds it will take to cross the wall.

WEB WEAVING

Equipment

Yarn or string—approximately 50 feet (15 meters) per climber

Description

In pairs, one partner holds the yarn while the other climbs on the wall. The non-climber follows and feeds yarn to the climber (spider). The spider moves around on the wall attaching the yarn to various handholds (figure 6.5). Changing directions will result in creative designs resembling a spider's web. The activity ends when the spider runs out of yarn.

Safety Considerations

Climbers should be instructed to use only handholds to create a web. Otherwise, reaching down to footholds places the climber off balance and greatly increases the chance of a fall.

Variations

- Increase or decrease the length of yarn.
- Establish a time limit; the next spider continues with the previous spider's web.
- Certain holds must be attempted, or avoided.
- Webs must involve a specified pattern (e.g., pentagon shape), or must include a specified number of places where the web crosses itself.

FIGURE 6.5 Web Weaving.

REHEARSING TRAVERSING (BOULDERING ACTIVITY)

Equipment

Tennis balls; masking tape; beanbags

Description

Climbers move across the wall, positioning their bodies in different ways. A climber who comes off the wall during a traverse may continue from that point. After completing a traverse, climbers assume the role of a spotter. To encourage climbers to work with both sides of the body, instructors should design activities where climbers will move from left to right, and also from right to left.

Safety Considerations

Climbers should be instructed not to rush or crowd another climber. Each climber should have at least one spotter at all times.

Variations

- Climbers must cross over hands or feet.
- Climbers must use the maximum (or minimum) number of holds; or, use all the holds in the bottom four or five rows with their feet.
- Climbers must make at least one foot change (or hand change) on the same hold.
- Climbers can use any handholds, but must move the trailing foot only to a hold beyond the leading foot (focuses climber's attention on footwork).
- Climbers do not use any holds that are blue (or some other color).
- Climbers use only the holds that are blue and red (or some other colors).
- Climbers use only holds that are marked with masking tape, or that are within pathways defined by masking tape (instructor can mark these in a wave pattern that suits the ability of the climbers; increasing the space between taped lines generally decreases the degree of difficulty).
- Climbers travel a predetermined distance, then retrace the route using exactly the same holds.
- Climbers carry a ball (switching from hand to hand is okay; this variation reduces reliance on hands and arms, placing more weight on feet and legs).
- Place beanbags below large holds. The challenge is for climbers to traverse to the beanbag, reach down and pick up the beanbag, and then place it onto a hold; the next climber reverses the activity (places the beanbag back on the ground).
- Climbers may use any holds, but only one hand (other hand kept behind back); at the end of a traverse, the climber may switch hands and try to return using the other hand.

COOPERATIVE CLIMBS (BOULDERING ACTIVITY)

Equipment
Eight-foot (243-centimeter) lengths of yarn; bandannas; hoops

Description
In pairs, climbers must travel together across the wall while attached to one another with yarn (figure 6.6). This requires climbers to slow down, to make more deliberate movements, and to plan ahead and communicate.

Safety Considerations
Increase the number of spotters for this activity.

Variations
- Another pair must traverse in the opposite direction, thus crisscrossing at some point.
- Using a shorter piece of yarn, loosely tie the left leg of one climber to the right leg of the other.
- Connected with yarn placed in their pockets, the challenge is for the most number of climbers to traverse without breaking the line (i.e., yarn pulled from someone's pocket).

FIGURE 6.6   Cooperative Climbs.

(continued)

- Next pair of climbers may not use any of the holds used by the previous pair.
- Next pair of climbers must use all of the holds used by the previous pair.
- Each pair of climbers may designate three holds that may not be used by the next pair.
- Lead climbers must support their blindfolded partners (or reverse roles by blindfolding the lead climber); this requires enhanced communication, planning, and dependence on kinesthetic perception.
- Instead of being connected with yarn, pairs must travel while both are holding a hoop (or two ends of a bandanna, or a Styrofoam tube).

RING MY CHIMES (BOULDERING ACTIVITY)

Equipment
Several bells; bandannas

Description
Climbers must traverse the wall from opposite ends and ring a bell that is attached to the wall. Each climber must ring the bell, signaling the end of his or her climb.

Safety Considerations
No special issues.

Variations
- Climbers must ring the bell with a specified body part (e.g., nose, elbow).
- Teams compete to ring the bell first; the next climber begins when the preceding teammate rings the bell.
- Add a second bell midway along each group's path; climbers must ring both bells, and ringing the first bell signals the next teammate to begin.
- Same as previous variation, but only one group is involved and tries for a personal best.
- Replace bells with bandannas or beanbags; the first climber retrieves an object, and the next climber replaces it.
- Climbers travel in pairs, attached to each other.

GHOST (BOULDERING ACTIVITY)

Equipment

None

Description

This adaptation of an old familiar elimination game requires participants to imitate another's moves. In this climbing wall version, climbers proceed in sequence, attempting to copy the movements of the first climber, who completes a traverse of several moves. The second climber must copy those moves and, if unsuccessful, acquires the letter *G*. Any subsequent climber who fails to copy the first climber's moves also acquires a *G*. After the first round, another player becomes the lead climber. The game ends when someone acquires all five letters, *GHOST*. As in any competition, the instructor should ensure that climbers are of similar ability (or should adjust the circumstances in order to avoid extremes in boredom or frustration).

Safety Considerations

No special issues.

Variations

- When a later climber fails to imitate the lead climber, instead of assigning a letter to that later climber (leading to possible elimination), a letter is awarded to the lead climber. The goal is to be first to achieve *GHOST.*
- In a group of four or five players, the first climber completes three moves; the second climber imitates those and adds two more; the third climber imitates those five, adds two more, and so on.
- Shorten or lengthen the word (e.g., *dog, carabiner*).
- Designate a point at which the lead climber must reverse direction.

PORTALS (BOULDERING ACTIVITY)

Equipment
Six to eight hoops attached to various holds (use duct tape or specially designed holds that clasp a hoop)

Description
Climbers traverse the wall while passing through a designated number of hoops (figure 6.7).

Safety Considerations
No special issues.

Variations
- Climbers follow one another ensuring that every hoop is passed through by at least one climber, and that every climber proceeds through at least one hoop.
- Following one another, climbers attempt to cross the entire wall without dislodging any hoops.
- Use different-sized hoops.
- Arrange some hoops vertically and others horizontally.
- Once someone ascends through a hoop, the next climber to use that hoop must descend through it.

FIGURE 6.7   Portals.

SMART ART (BOULDERING ACTIVITY)

Equipment

Colored chalk; small pieces of cardboard taped to the climbing wall

Description

Climbers traverse the wall and make marks (using chalk they carry with them) on each piece of cardboard they come to. To reduce reliance on hands and arms when climbing, climbers make marks on the pieces of cardboard while supporting themselves with both feet and only one hand.

Safety Considerations

Chalk should be easy to grasp and carry (pens and other sharp writing implements should be avoided).

Variations

- Climbers must write something or draw something.
- Climbers add to one another's writings or artwork.
- Instead of cardboard, use pages from coloring books.
- According to the directions on each piece of cardboard, climbers insert a noun or verb or adjective, and so on. Climbers later select words from the various pieces of cardboard to insert into a Mad Libs type of story (see example below).

Words needed to complete the story:

Adjective: _____

Adjective: _____

Plural noun: _____

Plural noun: _____

Number: _____

Adjective: _____

Adverb: _____

Plural noun: _____

Adjective: _____

Body part(s): _____

Body part(s): _____

Description of Our Climbing Group Today

We had a perfectly _____ADJECTIVE_____

time today at this _____ADJECTIVE_____ climbing wall.

The climbing wall is decorated with _____PLURAL NOUN_____

and with many stylish _____PLURAL NOUN_____

that must have cost at least _____NUMBER_____ dollars.

We are all _____ADJECTIVE_____ climbers

and are all _____ADVERB_____ dressed.

Most of us behave like angels, but once in a while

a few of us act like _____PLURAL NOUN_____.

Fortunately, our instructor is a dedicated and _____ADJECTIVE_____ teacher

who is trying to teach us to climb more with our _____BODY PARTS_____

and less with our _____BODY PARTS_____.

HIDDEN LETTERS

Equipment

Masking tape; small pieces of cardboard

Description

In pairs or small groups, climbers search for letters underneath pieces of cardboard that have been taped next to holds (figure 6.8). Some pieces of cardboard contain a letter, and others do not. Once a letter is discovered, the climber relays that information to a partner or teammate. The goal is to use letters to solve an anagram (e.g., climber is searching for the letters *C, O, R,* and *K*; partners must rearrange the letters to spell another word, in this case, *ROCK*).

FIGURE 6.8 Hidden Letters.

Safety Considerations

Stress the importance of perseverance and controlled movements rather than speed.

Variations

- Once one letter is located, another climber tries to locate the next letter.
- Color code pieces of cardboard that might contain vowels versus consonants.
- Provide some letters to begin with; climbers must locate the remaining letters.
- In place of anagrams, use words that must be inserted into a sentence (e.g., a five-letter word that completes the following sentence: "The climbing wall was covered with _ _ _ _ _." [holds, slime, hoops]).
- Instead of letters, use words (which must be combined and used in a sentence).
- Same as previous variation, but a discovered word must then be correctly used in a familiar poem (e.g., for *hill,* "Jack and Jill went up the hill") or as part of a class lesson (e.g., for *hill,* "Bunker Hill was the site of a famous battle during the American Revolution").
- Climbers attempt to locate as many letters as possible during a specified time period (e.g., five minutes per team); the team then uses all their letters to determine a word (much like the TV show "Wheel of Fortune"). To illustrate, a team locates the following letters: *E, L, M, J,* and *R.* They must discover a word by inserting letters into the following: B _ _ A _ _ _. By inserting *E, L,* and *R* (*M* and *J* are not used), they arrive at B E L A _ E R and discover the word *BELAYER.*

THE ART OF CLIMBING (BOULDERING ACTIVITY)

Equipment
Colored electrical tape or masking tape

Description
Climbers carry a dozen or so pieces of tape and place them on the wall in order to create a temporary piece of art (figure 6.9). Each climber must add to the previous climber's artwork.

Safety Considerations
No special issues.

Variations
- In pairs or small groups, "artists" must decide beforehand their art project (e.g., a large star, clock, or windmill), and then plan and execute accordingly.
- Small groups work collaboratively on a theme (e.g., "winter delights" might involve snowflakes, a snowman, and skates or sleds).
- Using an overhead projector, cast a design or object onto the wall. Climbers must use the projected image as a basis for their artwork.
- One group creates a piece of abstract art while another group must uncover its meaning (e.g., the Olympics) or guess the artist (e.g., Picasso).

FIGURE 6.9 **The Art of Climbing.**

THE GAMBLER

Equipment

Dice (large Styrofoam blocks work well, but dice can also be easily constructed from small square boxes); pieces of masking tape with numbers written on them (attached to the wall at various locations)

Description

Each time the dice are rolled, a climber proceeds to a piece of masking tape that equals the sum of the dice.

Safety Considerations

In variations that involve competition, stress the importance of controlled, deliberate climbing (perhaps subtracting points for falls or slips) and ensure that climbers do not interfere with one another.

Variations

- Use a spinner in place of the dice.
- Climbers continue to climb until a particular sum is reached (e.g., 50).
- Two or more climbers attempt to reach a particular sum first. In this variation, sections of the wall can be separated according to degree of difficulty (e.g., in a more difficult section, fewer holds contain numbers; in a simpler section, every hold has at least one number, with several holds having more than one number).
- Climbers move only to odd- or even-numbered holds, attempting 15 total moves.
- Climbers may choose to add or to subtract each roll (e.g., a roll of 3 and 4 could be selected as 7 by adding 3 + 4, or could be selected as 1 by subtracting 4 − 3).
- Omit use of the dice. Each handhold is numbered. As a climber traverses the wall, a partner jots down the number attached to every fifth handhold that the climber uses. These numbers are entered on a math task card that the climber must complete following the climb.

CATEGORIES

Equipment

Masking tape; small pieces of cardboard, some of which have characteristics of one of four types of traditional Native American homes (Pueblo adobe, Arctic igloo, Northwest plank house, Central Plains tepee) written on the back; one sheet of paper per group, listing the four home types

Description

In small groups, climbers search for characteristics underneath pieces of cardboard that have been taped next to holds. Once a characteristic is discovered, the group writes that characteristic under the appropriate heading. For example, "no trees" would be included under "Arctic igloo," whereas "large trees" might be included under "Northwest plank house." Other characteristics might include living habits (nomad, settled), rain (large amounts, little), climate (hot, very cold), or food source (hunting, farming, fishing). Some characteristics might be shared (hunters), while others may be exclusive (very cold climate). The goal is to correctly identify at least five characteristics for each of the four categories.

Safety Considerations

No special issues.

Variations

- Use other classifications, which may include types of trees (bark, buds, flowers, fruit); life zones in the Rocky Mountains such as alpine, subalpine, montane, foothills, and plains (altitude, annual rainfall, trees); or life forms such as mammal, bird, reptile, and amphibian.
- A climber must find a second characteristic for a given category before being allowed to locate a characteristic that matches a different one. For instance, in the life forms example, suppose a climber locates "constant body temperature," and the group places it under the category "mammal." The climber then uncovers "has feathers." Because the group did not place "constant body temperature" under the category "birds" (which also would have been correct), they cannot use that characteristic until the climber first uncovers another characteristic for the "mammal" category.
- Some groups receive fewer or more categories than other groups (e.g., one group receives lizard, seagull, and bear while another group receives those as well as chipmunk and bat; or one group receives food and shelter while another group also receives prey).
- Award points. For example, after correctly locating three characteristics in any given category, a point is awarded for each additional characteristic in that category.
- Impose penalties. For example, incorrectly classifying a characteristic costs the group a point. If penalties are imposed, ensure that the penalties do not detract from the enjoyment of climbing (e.g., each penalty requires pull-ups or traverses, which is tantamount to push-ups and wind sprints—associating physical activity with punishment).

HOT SPOTS

Equipment

Colored tape for marking holds

Description

Before the climbing session, use different colors of tape to mark at least one-third of the holds with interspersed colors. First, pairs of climbers select a hold color. Any holds marked with that color cannot be used as they traverse or climb a route. Next, pairs identify and attempt a route. Their goal is to complete the route without touching any "hot" holds.

Safety Considerations

For variations in which a climber might remain on the wall for long periods of time (e.g., moving back and forth between holds that are far from one another), reserve the right to intercede and give the climber some reasonable recovery time.

Variations

- Points are given for each "hot" hold touched and for stepping off the climb; the goal is to collect the fewest points.
- Same as previous variation, but points accrue over five attempts by each climber; or, count the best four of each climber's five attempts; or only each climber's best climb (i.e., lowest score) counts.
- Climbers must navigate the "hot" holds within a specified time period.
- Same as previous variation, but rather than avoiding "hot" holds, climbers must use all of them during their timed attempts.
- Allow climbers to reposition colors, either for themselves or for their competitors.
- Replace colors with numbers (1 to 6). One partner rolls a die, and the other must climb to that number. After the climber touches that number, the partner rolls again, and the climber must now move to the new number. Partners switch roles when the climber successfully touches 10 numbers in sequence.

Summary

We hope that these sample activities and variations help to generate enthusiasm and excitement in your climbing program. Also, by providing you with strategies for modifying activities and creating your own activities, we trust that every new twist that you add to your program's activities will result in enhanced and sustained interest among your climbing wall's participants.

Appendix A

Sample Forms and Checklists

Climbing Wall Orientation Outline

Date and time of session: _____

Supervisor name(s): _____

1. SAFETY

☐ Discuss safety guidelines for the wall, emphasizing key safety issues.

2. CONSENT

☐ Distribute and discuss the Informed Consent form and the Belay Certification card.

☐ Explain where these are stored and the check-in procedure for each visit to the wall.

☐ Ask patrons to complete the front side of the Informed Consent form and to return it immediately to you.

3. CHECKOUT

☐ Explain how and where to check out shoes, harnesses, and belay devices; front desk staff will require patrons to present their individual belay card.

4. HARNESS

☐ Describe and demonstrate how to properly fit and secure a harness.

☐ Ask each patron to put on a harness. Supervisor should check fit, buckles, and double passing through.

5. TIE-IN

☐ Demonstrate the proper technique for tying into a harness.

☐ After demonstrating, observe each patron demonstrate correct tie-in procedure.

6. BELAYING

☐ Discuss belay check requirements (i.e., belay certification).

☐ Explain that each patron, prior to belaying, must receive instructions from our staff.

☐ Inform patrons of the days and times that belay schools are offered.

☐ Inform patrons of safety checks that should be performed prior to each climb (belayer's harness and belay devices, climber's harness and tie-in, and so on).

(continued)

From *Climbing Walls: A Complete Guide* by Jim Stiehl and Tim B. Ramsey, 2005, Champaign, IL: Human Kinetics.

Climbing Wall Orientation Outline *(continued)*

7. ADDITIONAL

☐ Provide information about the climbing room in general, and about specific routes.

☐ Inform patrons that climbing on an indoor wall does not provide them with the skills or knowledge required for climbing or bouldering outdoors. Those who choose to climb outdoors should seek instruction that is designed specifically for outdoor climbing (e.g., courses through the School of Sport and Exercise Science).

☐ Inform patrons that a maximum of 18 climbers are permitted in the climbing room (maintaining a supervisor to patron ratio of 1:6).

☐ Advise patrons to always lower climbers slowly.

☐ Identify which belay bars to use on specific routes.

☐ Point out the marking of routes.

☐ Point out ceiling structure and wall supports, which must not be touched.

☐ Warn patrons to never walk on ropes.

☐ Explain the importance of sharing time on routes. Is anyone waiting?

☐ Advise patrons that no food, no drinks, and no excess gear are permitted in the climbing room.

☐ Other (list pertinent information, questions, or concerns):

From *Climbing Walls: A Complete Guide* by Jim Stiehl and Tim B. Ramsey, 2005, Champaign, IL: Human Kinetics.

Climber Checklist

Instructions: These skills must be successfully completed to use the climbing wall.

Skills   **Comments**

Harness

- ☐ Worn properly
- ☐ Fits snugly
- ☐ Belt buckle doubled back
- ☐ Leg straps doubled back

Climber setup

- ☐ Tied directly into harness
- ☐ Tied in using a figure eight follow-through knot
- ☐ Double fisherman's knot as backup
- ☐ Double checks belayer setup

Belayer setup

- ☐ Harness worn correctly
- ☐ Belay device used correctly
- ☐ Carabiner oriented lengthwise and locked
- ☐ Demonstrates correct use of anchor
- ☐ Double checks climber setup

Climber commands

- ☐ Knows appropriate use of belay commands
- ☐ Establishes "on belay" before climbing

Belaying

- ☐ Belayer demonstrates safe and consistent technique
- ☐ Brake hand never leaves rope
- ☐ Belayer keeps rope taut
- ☐ Uses proper lowering techniques
- ☐ Catches an announced fall
- ☐ Catches an unannounced fall

(continued)

From *Climbing Walls: A Complete Guide* by Jim Stiehl and Tim B. Ramsey, 2005, Champaign, IL: Human Kinetics.
Adapted from Slippery Rock University and North Carolina State University guidelines.

Climber Checklist *(continued)*

Overall grade
☐ Pass
☐ Fail
☐ Retest

Name (print) _____

Signature _____

Date _____

Instructor signature _____

Date _____

From *Climbing Walls: A Complete Guide* by Jim Stiehl and Tim B. Ramsey, 2005, Champaign, IL: Human Kinetics.
Adapted from Slippery Rock University and North Carolina State University guidelines.

Belay Card

☐ **Boulder only.** Check this box if you will ONLY be bouldering at the campus climbing wall. Complete your orientation session with the climbing wall supervisor. Sign the risk statement on the reverse side of this card.

COMPLETED ORIENTATION SESSION

Date	Time	Instructor Name(s)
_____	_____	_____

Belay information:

☐ Initial instruction _____

    Comments _____

_____

    Instructor name _____

☐ 2nd belay check _____

    Comments _____

_____

    Instructor name _____

☐ 3rd belay check _____

    Comments _____

_____

    Instructor name _____

Boulderers and climbers: Please record the number of times you come in to climb during the year.

From *Climbing Walls: A Complete Guide* by Jim Stiehl and Tim B. Ramsey, 2005, Champaign, IL: Human Kinetics.

Climbing Wall Instruction Acknowledgment

Please read the following information and check the box affirming that you understand each statement. If any of the information is not clear to you or you do not understand, ask your instructor for clarifications. It is important that you read this thoroughly.

- ☐ I was instructed how to properly put on a harness.
- ☐ I was instructed how to properly tie a figure eight follow-through knot.
- ☐ I was instructed how to feed the rope through the attachment point(s) on the harness.
- ☐ I was instructed how to properly tie a double fisherman's knot.
- ☐ I was instructed how to use the carabiner properly.
- ☐ I was instructed how to use the belaying device.
- ☐ I was instructed on the importance of the brake hand. I understand that I must keep my brake hand on the rope at all times.
- ☐ I was instructed on the proper commands to be used when climbing and belaying.

Name (print) _____

Signature _____

Date _____

Instructor signature _____

Date _____

Informed Consent/Acknowledgment of Risk/Agreement to Participate

Round Rocks Climbing Wall

Square Pegs School

I am aware that participating in climbing or wall climbing can be a dangerous activity involving many risks of injury. I understand that such risks simply cannot be eliminated without jeopardizing the essential qualities of the activity. The risks include, among other things, climbing on, or falling off, loose or damaged artificial holds; falling to the ground or onto other participants, or being fallen on by other participants; abrasions from the walls, ropes, or the floor; equipment failure, belay failure, or climbing out of control or beyond one's personal limits; and the negligence of other climbers, visitors, participants, or other persons who may be present, or my own negligence.

I understand that the dangers and risks of participating in wall climbing include, but are not limited to, death, serious neck and spinal injuries (which may result in paralysis), and serious injury or impairment to other aspects of my body, general health, and well-being. I understand that the dangers and risks involved in wall climbing may result not only in serious injury but also in a serious impairment of my future abilities to earn a living; to engage in other business, social, and recreational activities; and to enjoy life in general.

Because of the potential dangers of participating in wall climbing, I recognize the importance of following the supervisor's instructions regarding belaying, climbing, and wall rules. Moreover, I agree to adhere to such instructions.

I have read and understand the aforementioned safety policies regarding the indoor climbing wall. I hereby assume all the risks associated with participation and agree to hold Square Pegs School, its employees, agent's representatives, and volunteers harmless from any and all liabilities. If I do not understand, I will ask for further explanation from a staff member so that I can clearly understand each policy and what is expected of me.

Name _____

(please print)

Signature _____ Date _____

Signature of parent or guardian _____

(if under 18)

Date _____

From *Climbing Walls: A Complete Guide* by Jim Stiehl and Tim B. Ramsey, 2005, Champaign, IL: Human Kinetics. Adapted from UNC Rec Center.

Climbing Wall Participants' Agreement for School Groups

I, the undersigned, as authorized representative of _____
_____, hereafter referred to as the "Group," request use of the climbing wall and accept full responsibility for the safety of all participants from the Group while on and around the climbing wall. I agree to abide by and enforce the following Safety Policies:

- A signed Climbing Wall Participant's Agreement and Safety Policy Contract for each participant must be on file at John Doe Middle School.
- The climbing wall manager will be informed of any situation seen as unsafe or not in accordance with these safety policies. All accidents or equipment damage will be reported immediately to the climbing wall manager.
- The Group must supply at least 1 adult supervisor for every 10 members of the Group. Group supervisors are responsible for maintaining order and ensuring all directions given by the climbing wall manager are obeyed.
- All members of the Group must adhere to the climbing wall manager's directions regarding technique, training, safety, equipment use, and other stated rules.
- Individuals within the Group may be assigned to a smaller unit during instruction and stay with that unit.
- If any Group member's behavior is distracting to others or is unsafe in any manner, that person or the entire Group may be restricted from continued participation in climbing activities.
- Individuals within the Group may share views or may have different skill levels. "Put-downs" or teasing will not be tolerated.
- Individuals within the Group may be assigned responsibility of spotting other climbers. This is an extremely important activity that must be taken seriously to protect the well-being of both the spotter and the climber involved.
- A positive and cooperative attitude must be maintained by all members of the Group at all times.

The climbing wall manager and the school reserve the right to deny to any individual (permanently or for a specified period of time) access to the school's facilities if any individual or Group fails to follow these safety policies, or for any conduct that is deemed unsafe or inappropriate.

I acknowledge that I have read and agree to abide by and enforce these safety policies with every member of my Group.

_____

Representative's signature/date

_____

Group/agency name

From *Climbing Walls: A Complete Guide* by Jim Stiehl and Tim B. Ramsey, 2005, Champaign, IL: Human Kinetics.

Climbing Wall Release/Indemnification of All Claims and Covenant Not to Sue

Notice: This is a legally binding agreement. By signing this agreement, you give up your right to bring a court action to recover compensation or to obtain other remedy for any injury to yourself or your property or for your death however caused arising out of your use of the climbing wall, now or any time in the future.

Acknowledgment of Risk

I hereby acknowledge and agree that the sport of rock climbing and the use of the climbing wall have inherent risks. I have full knowledge of the nature and extent of all the risks associated with rock climbing and the use of the climbing wall, including but not limited to the following:

1. All manner of injury resulting from falling off the climbing wall and hitting the floor or hitting rock faces and projections whether permanently or temporarily in place.
2. Rope abrasion, injuries caused by entanglement, and other injuries resulting from activities on or near the climbing wall, such as, but not limited to, climbing, belaying, rappelling, lowering on the rope, rescue systems, and any other rope techniques.
3. Injuries resulting from falling climbers or dropping items, such as, but not limited to, ropes or climbing hardware.
4. Cuts and abrasions resulting from skin contact with the wall.
5. Failure of the rope, slings, harnesses, climbing hardware, anchor points, or any part of the wall.

I further acknowledge that the above list is not inclusive of all possible risks associated with the use of the climbing wall and that the above list in no way limits the extent or reach of this release and covenant not to sue.

Release/Indemnification and Covenant Not to Sue

In consideration of my use of the climbing wall, I _____, the undersigned user, agree to release and on behalf of myself, my heirs, representatives, executors, administrators, and assigns, hereby do release *Roy's Rock Gym*, its officers, agents, and employees from any cause of action, claim, or demand of any nature whatsoever, including but not limited to a claim of negligence, which I, my heirs, representatives, executors, administrators, and assigns may now have, or have in the future, against *Roy's Rock Gym* on account of personal injury, property damage, death, or accident of any kind arising out of or in any way related to my use of the climbing wall, whether that use is supervised or unsupervised, however the injury or damage is caused, including, but not limited to the negligence of *Roy's Rock Gym,* its officers, agents, and employees.

(continued)

Climbing Wall Release/Indemnification of All Claims and Covenant Not to Sue *(continued)*

In consideration of my use of the climbing wall, I, the undersigned user, agree to indemnify and hold harmless *Roy's Rock Gym*, its officers, agents, and employees from any and all causes of action, claims, demands, losses, or costs of any nature whatsoever arising out of or in any way related to my use of the climbing wall.

I hereby certify that I have full knowledge of the nature and extent of the risks inherent in the use of the climbing wall and that I am voluntarily assuming those risks. I understand that I will be solely responsible for any loss or damage, including death, I sustain while using the climbing wall and that by this agreement, I am relieving *Roy's Rock Gym* of any and all liability for such loss, damage, or death.

I further certify that I am in good health and that I have no physical limitations that would preclude my safe use of the wall.

I further certify that my date of birth is _____(month/day/year), that my present age is _____, and that I am therefore of lawful age (18 years or older) and otherwise legally competent to sign this agreement. I understand that the terms of this agreement are legally binding, and I certify that I am signing this agreement, after I have carefully read it, of my own free will.

_____

Name   Date

Helmet Waiver

I, the undersigned, recognize that participating in wall climbing can be a dangerous activity involving many risks of injury. I also understand that such risks simply cannot be eliminated without jeopardizing the essential qualities of the activity.

I have been offered use of a protective helmet, which, in the event of an accident, could prevent permanent brain damage. Against the advice of Campus Wall staff, and the insurance company, I am refusing this critical safety precaution.

_____

Climber must write "I have read and understand the above"

_____

Climber signature (if under 18, parent or guardian signature)

From *Climbing Walls: A Complete Guide* by Jim Stiehl and Tim B. Ramsey, 2005, Champaign, IL: Human Kinetics.

Bouldering Wall Safety Policies

I, the undersigned user of John Doe Middle School Climbing Wall, accept full responsibility for my own safety and will respect the safety of other participants while on or around the climbing wall. I agree to abide by the following safety policies:

- I have signed the Climbing Wall Participant's Agreement, and it is on file at John Doe Middle School.
- I will inform the teacher of any situation seen as unsafe or not in accordance with these safety policies.
- I recognize the importance of following the teacher's directions regarding technique, training, safety, equipment use, and other rules; and I agree to obey such directions.
- I understand that I may be assigned to a group during instruction, and I agree to stay with that group.
- I understand that if my behavior is distracting to others or is unsafe in any manner, I may be restricted from continued participation in climbing activities.
- I agree to report any injury, no matter how minor, immediately to the instructor or other staff member.
- I respect that individuals may have views that differ from mine or may have different skill levels than mine. I agree that I will not use "put-downs" toward others or myself.
- I accept the responsibility of spotting and the high expectations of safety related to climbing.
- I recognize the importance of a positive attitude, and I agree to give my best efforts on each day's activities.

The teacher and the school reserve the right to deny to any individual (permanently or for a specified period of time) access to the school's facilities if that individual fails to follow these safety policies, or for any conduct that is deemed unsafe or inappropriate.

Your signature below indicates that you understand the above safety policies and agree to abide by them.

_____

Participant's signature/date

_____

Parent's signature/date

From *Climbing Walls: A Complete Guide* by Jim Stiehl and Tim B. Ramsey, 2005, Champaign, IL: Human Kinetics.
Adapted from NOCO Climbing Wall Operations Guidelines and Sate University of New York College at Cortland Outdoor Education Practicum Staff Manual.

Climbing Wall Safety Policies

Because climbing styles and procedures vary, our college has adopted the following policies for its indoor climbing facility. The purpose of these policies is to provide a safe, friendly, and encouraging climbing atmosphere.

1. The climbing facility is not to be used without a climbing supervisor on duty.

2. Patrons must sign an Informed Consent form before using the facility. Those under the age of 18 must have a parent or guardian signature on this form before climbing. Minors must be accompanied by an adult during recreational climbing times.

3. No one is to climb above the designated height of eight feet without being tied into a rope, with a belay.

4. Bouldering must occur below the designated eight-foot line and must not interfere with roped climbers or belayers (e.g., no bouldering under climbers).

5. Only those who have passed a competency evaluation by a climbing wall supervisor may belay a climber. Beginners must attend an orientation session, while experienced climbers may demonstrate belay skills to a supervisor. To qualify for a belay check, the patron must demonstrate how to
   - properly fit an approved harness (including *doubling back* through the buckle, if recommended by the manufacturer);
   - tie directly into the harness according to manufacturer's recommendations using a properly tied *figure eight follow-through* knot (with at least a six-inch tail);
   - give and respond to the appropriate belay commands; and
   - perform safe belay skills including belay setup, taking in rope, catching falls, and controlled lowering.

6. Before each climb, patrons must use the *buddy system* to double-check harness buckles, knots, and belay setups:
   a. Climber and belayer check themselves individually.
   b. Belayer checks climber (e.g., tightness, doubled back, knots tied correctly, and tied into rope closest to wall).
   c. Climber checks belayer (e.g., doubled back, carabiner locked down, and belay device set up properly).

7. In the event of a disagreement, patrons should ask a supervisor to perform the final check.

(continued)

From *Climbing Walls: A Complete Guide* by Jim Stiehl and Tim B. Ramsey, 2005, Champaign, IL: Human Kinetics.

Climbing Wall Safety Policies *(continued)*

8. To avoid possible injuries and interference while climbing, patrons must remove any inappropriate jewelry (e.g., dangling earrings, long necklaces, large belt buckles) and hats that may get caught on holds or in the belay system.

9. Only climbing shoes or athletic footwear are allowed on the wall (no open toe or open heel). Care should be taken to tuck in loose clothing and to tie back long hair that could become entangled in equipment. Clothing should be comfortable and allow a full range of movement.

10. Harnesses and shoes are the only personal equipment climbers may use on the climbing wall. All equipment must be inspected and approved by a supervisor before climbing. Supervisors have the authority to disallow the use of questionable gear.

11. Patrons must be alert to indoor climbing hazards such as falling or swinging climbers, objects on the floor, and overuse injuries. Do not climb above the anchors or interfere with lighting, pipes, or other fixtures. Although the staff conducts regular safety inspections within the facility, each patron has a responsibility to point out possible safety concerns to a climbing wall staff member.

From *Climbing Walls: A Complete Guide* by Jim Stiehl and Tim B. Ramsey, 2005, Champaign, IL: Human Kinetics.

Climbing Wall Maintenance Checklist

School _____   Wall type _____

Inspector name _____   Date _____

☐ 1. Inspect routes at the beginning of each day, and correct any deficiencies:

    ❏ a. Missing or faulty route markers.

    ❏ b. Buildup of chalk or rubber residue. If necessary, remove and wash holds.

☐ 2. During route replacement, strip ALL holds and do the following:

    ❏ a. Clean holds until free of chalk and rubber residue.

    ❏ b. Inspect holds, replacing damaged holds or filing off sharp edges. Damaged holds may be eligible for warranty replacement by manufacturers.

    ❏ c. Save any broken holds, and maintain a written log of broken or faulty holds.

☐ 3. During route setting, mark damaged T-nuts. At the earliest reasonable opportunity, or at scheduled intervals, replace damaged T-nuts.

☐ 4. When belay bars are used, top ropes must wrap around the bar one complete turn. A complete wrap increases friction substantially, thereby increasing the margin of safety.

☐ 5. Report any accident or near miss incident involving district equipment (use an Equipment Incident Report form). Any equipment that may have sustained damage MUST be IMMEDIATELY removed from use and secured by the climbing wall supervisor.

    ❏ a. Equipment that may not be in safe operating condition MUST be destroyed or returned to its manufacturer. Record the disposition of such equipment using the Equipment Incident Report.

    ❏ b. If the climbing wall supervisor determines the equipment to be in proper working order, and returns it to active use, this must be noted in the report.

    ❏ c. Equipment that must be inspected after any accident or near miss includes the following:

        ❏ (1) Ropes. If the sheath is damaged to the point where the core is visible, the rope should be replaced. Any exposure to chemical contamination is also cause for replacement.

        ❏ (2) Quickdraws.

        ❏ (3) Bolt hanger plates.

        ❏ (4) Floor belay anchors.

        ❏ (5) Helmets.

        ❏ (6) Belay devices and carabiners.

        ❏ (7) Harnesses.

(continued)

From *Climbing Walls: A Complete Guide* by Jim Stiehl and Tim B. Ramsey, 2005, Champaign, IL: Human Kinetics.

Climbing Wall Maintenance Checklist *(continued)*

☐ 6. Log all maintenance activity after its completion using the appropriate Inspection Report and checklist. Items to be inspected include the following:

    ❏ a. Daily

        ❏ (1) Lead ropes

        ❏ (2) Top ropes

        ❏ (3) Rental harnesses

        ❏ (4) Rental belay gear

        ❏ (5) Rental helmets

        ❏ (6) Floor belay anchors

        ❏ (7) Quickdraws

    ❏ b. Monthly

        ❏ (1) Belay bars and attachments

        ❏ (2) Top-rope guide slings and attachments

        ❏ (3) Bolt hangars and their backing supports

        ❏ (4) Floor belay anchor attachments

        ❏ (5) Wall panel attachment (from rear)

        ❏ (6) Support beam attachment (from rear)

        ❏ (7) Wall surface texture (loosening, cracking)

        ❏ (8) Landing zone material integrity

_____

Signature of inspector

Date _____

_____

Signature of climbing wall manager

Date _____

From *Climbing Walls: A Complete Guide* by Jim Stiehl and Tim B. Ramsey, 2005, Champaign, IL: Human Kinetics.

Climbing Wall Equipment Incident Report

Date _____

School _____   Participant name(s) _____

Problem reported:

Equipment affected and nature of potential damage:

Inspection conducted:
Initial:

Disposition of equipment:
Initial:

_____

Signature of authorized instructor

Date _____

_____

Signature of climbing wall manager

Date _____

From *Climbing Walls: A Complete Guide* by Jim Stiehl and Tim B. Ramsey, 2005, Champaign, IL: Human Kinetics.

Climbing Wall Inspection Checklist

School _____   Wall type _____

Inspector name _____   Date of inspection _____

- [ ] 1. Accurate records are maintained of purchase dates and use characteristics of all safety-related equipment.
- [ ] 2. Daily inspections are conducted of all safety-related equipment.
- [ ] 3. First aid kit is adequately stocked. Anything missing is being replaced or is on order.
- [ ] 4. Supply of waivers is adequate. Copies are being made if supply is low.
- [ ] 5. Harnesses checked for damage or unusual wear. Replace as needed.*
- [ ] 6. Helmets checked for damage or unusual wear. Replace as needed.*
- [ ] 7. Anchors checked for damage or unusual wear. Replace as needed.*
- [ ] 8. Ropes handle well and do not appear worn or damaged. Replace as needed.
- [ ] 9. Belay devices and carabiners checked for damage or unusual wear. Replace as needed.*
- [ ] 10. Holds are tight and do not rotate or cause damage to the wall. Holds themselves are not damaged.
- [ ] 11. All wall panels were visually inspected for damaged or loose fasteners.
- [ ] 12. Wall was inspected for any damaged or splintered plywood or supports.
- [ ] 13. There is no visible damage to the climbing wall.
- [ ] 14. Landing zone surface material is adequate for the height of the wall.
- [ ] 15. Belay anchor or bar, and fittings or fasteners, were visually inspected for damage or unusual wear.
- [ ] 16. Arrangements are made for periodic inspections of structural fasteners attaching to the existing building.
- [ ] 17. Arrangements are made for periodic inspections of any roof abnormality that might lead to damage of the climbing wall or structural attachments to the existing building.
- [ ] 18. Any damage or needed repairs are immediately reported to the wall supervisor or safety officer.
- [ ] 19. Agreements or contracts for all classes are maintained for the duration of the class. At a session's end, all expired agreements or contracts are submitted to the wall supervisor or safety officer.

(continued)

Climbing Wall Inspection Checklist *(continued)*

☐ 20. Records of all safety inspections are maintained at the facility. Copies of monthly and yearly safety inspections are submitted to the appropriate district officials.

Signature of inspector _____

Date _____

Signature of climbing wall manager _____

Date _____

* Refer to manufacturer's specifications and recommendations.

Climbing Wall Inspection Report

Date _____   Staff member _____

Last inspection date _____

- Circle number upon passing inspection.
- Note problems and failed pieces in spaces provided.
- Check space provided upon completion of each area inspected.

FRONT OF WALL

_____	**Ropes:**	1 2 3 4 5 6 7 8 9 10 11 12
_____	**Harnesses:**	1 2 3 4 5 6 7 8 9 10 11 12
_____	**Carabiners:**	
_____	**Belay devices:**	1 2 3 4 5 6 7 8 9 10 11 12
_____	**Slings:**	
_____	**Top-rope belay anchors:**	
_____	**Lead climb protection anchors:**	
_____	**Holds:**	
_____	**Chips, cracks, flakes:**	

FLOOR

_____	**Cushioning surface:**	_____
_____	**Belay anchors:**	_____
_____	**Daisy chains:**	_____

BACK OF WALL

_____	**Anchor welds:**	
_____	**Chains:**	
_____	**Structural welds:**	

From *Climbing Walls: A Complete Guide* by Jim Stiehl and Tim B. Ramsey, 2005, Champaign, IL: Human Kinetics.
Adapted from Slippery Rock University Climbing Procedures Manual.

Climbing Wall Daily Inspection Report and Checklist

School _____   Wall type _____

Inspector name _____   Date _____

Initial upon completing each category.

_____   Lead ropes

_____   Top ropes

_____   Rental harnesses

_____   Rental belay gear

_____   Rental helmets

_____   Floor belay anchors

_____   Quickdraws

Problems observed:
Actions taken:

Climbing Wall Monthly Inspection Report and Checklist

School _____ Wall type _____

Inspector name _____ Date _____

Initial upon completing each category.

_____ Belay bars and attachments

_____ Top-rope guide slings and attachments

_____ Bolt hangers and their backing plates

_____ Floor belay anchor attachments (bolts)

_____ Wall panel attachment (from rear)

_____ Support beam attachment (from rear)

_____ Wall surface texturing (for loosening, spalling, or cracking)

_____ Landing zone material

Problems observed:

Actions taken:

Accident or Incident Report

Name of participant _____ Gender: M F Age _____

Check applicable categories:

Injury _____   Illness _____   Near miss* _____   Other incident _____

* A near miss is an accident that has the potential for serious injury, although a minor or no injury occurred.

Date of incident/accident _____ Time _____ (A.M., P.M.)

Type of injury:

_____ Abrasion   _____ Fracture

_____ Concussion   _____ Laceration

_____ Contusion   _____ Sprain

_____ Dental   _____ Strain

_____ Dislocation

_____ Other: _____

Activity:

_____ Bouldering   _____ Top-rope climbing

_____ Belaying   _____ Observing

_____ Other: _____

Witnesses (list specific witnesses of accident/incident):

_____

_____

Immediate cause:

_____ Exceeding ability   _____ Improper equipment

_____ Exhaustion   _____ Improper supervision

_____ Failure to follow   _____ Improper technique
                instructions

_____ Fall   Other: _____

_____ Falling object

(continued)

Accident or Incident Report *(continued)*

List all gear/equipment involved: _____

_____

Route in use: _____

Narrative (factually describe how the accident or incident happened; include medical treatment given and disposition of the patient):

_____

_____

_____

_____

Analysis (include any recommendations, suggestions, and observations):

_____

_____

_____

_____

Report submitted by _____   Date_____

Comments by climbing wall supervisor:

_____

_____

_____

_____

_____

Signature of supervisor _____   Date_____

Rope Inspection Log

Rope #	QUALITY OF ROPE (Check all that apply)				Replace? (Y/N; date replaced)	Initial/Date
	Dirty (cleaned?)	Fuzzy (core visible?)	Flat spot (where—middle, end?)	Kink (where?)		

(continued)

Rope Inspection Log *(continued)*

Retirement Criteria:

There continues to be no hard-and-fast rule as to when to retire a rope. How long your ropes last will depend on the amount and type of use and how well you take care of them. The following are accepted manufacturer's retirement guidelines:

Retire a climbing wall rope . . .

1. when there may be damage (examples include possible chemical contamination, extensive sheath slippage or abrasion as in a "fuzzy" rope, exposed core, glazing, or irregularity in the core such as soft, hollow, or lumpy, or any lack of uniform diameter);
2. after several years (frequently cited as no more than five years after its manufacture date, even if unused); or
3. if you have a loss of confidence in the rope (could include suspicion of how the rope was washed, whether it might have been tampered with, or when its look or feel is unnerving for any unexplained reason).

From *Climbing Walls: A Complete Guide* by Jim Stiehl and Tim B. Ramsey, 2005, Champaign, IL: Human Kinetics.

Carabiner and Belay Device Inspection Log

Equipment number	Condition	Checked by	Date

Quickdraw and Anchor Inspection Log

Equipment number	Condition	Checked by	Date

From *Climbing Walls: A Complete Guide* by Jim Stiehl and Tim B. Ramsey, 2005, Champaign, IL: Human Kinetics.

Harness Inspection Log

Equipment number	Condition	Checked by	Date

From *Climbing Walls: A Complete Guide* by Jim Stiehl and Tim B. Ramsey, 2005, Champaign, IL: Human Kinetics.

Climbing Shoe Inspection Log

Equipment number	Condition	Checked by	Date

From *Climbing Walls: A Complete Guide* by Jim Stiehl and Tim B. Ramsey, 2005, Champaign, IL: Human Kinetics.

Sample First Aid Kit Contents

This first aid kit is designed for use with 10 persons or fewer. It exceeds OSHA regulations, though state laws may vary. First aid kits should be repacked periodically (check any expiration dates, damaged items, and so on).

Contents:

- (16) 3/4 × 3 in. adhesive plastic bandages
- (1) 2 × 4 in. elbow and knee plastic bandage
- (1) 1-3/4 × 2 in. small fingertip fabric bandage
- (4) 2 × 2 in. gauze dressing pads (2 packs of 2)
- (4) 3 × 3 in. gauze dressing pads (2 packs of 2)
- (2) 4 × 4 in. gauze dressing pads (1 pack of 2)
- (1) 5 × 9 in. trauma pad
- (1) 2 in. × 4.1 yd conforming gauze roll bandage
- (1) 3 in. × 4.1 yd conforming gauze roll bandage
- (1) triangular sling/bandage
- (1) 6 × 9 in. instant cold compress
- (2) exam quality gloves (1 pair)
- (1) sterile eye pad
- (3) triple antibiotic ointment packs
- (1) burn relief pack (3.5 grams)
- (6) alcohol cleansing pads
- (6) antiseptic cleansing wipes (sting free)
- (1) 1 in. × 5 yd first aid tape roll
- (6) aspirin tablets (3 packs of 2)
- (1) 4-1/2 in. scissors, nickel plated
- (1) 4-in. tweezers, plastic
- (1) first aid guide
- (1) CPR mask/shield

Rescue Belay Policy

Due to the nature of the belay system, it would be very rare for a rope or climber to become trapped or jammed on the climbing wall (e.g., caught on holds or hangers). Nonetheless, all supervisors should be familiar with the following policy and procedures.

In the event of an emergency where a belayer cannot lower a climber, or where it is determined unsafe to lower a climber, follow these steps:

1. The supervisor should call "STOP" to all climbing parties, and then calmly inform everyone of the situation and the course of action being taken.
2. The supervisor will go to the belayer and either assist the belayer or take over for the belayer and lower the climber.

NOTE: A trauma scissors is located in the first aid kit and should only be used to cut clothing or hair, NOT the climbing rope. Be sure to pull as much slack from the rope as possible and to keep your hand on the brake while cutting clothing or hair. The trauma scissors should only be used as a last resort in any situation.

If it is determined that the climber *cannot be lowered safely* by the supervisor, the following plan will be implemented:

1. The supervisor should call "STOP" to all climbing parties, and then calmly inform everyone of the situation and the course of action being taken.
2. The supervisor should assign a staff member to move parties that are not involved away from the area.
3. The supervisor should appoint a staff member to notify the building manager of the situation.
4. The supervisor should assign available staff members to bring an extension ladder (located in the storage room behind the front desk) to the climbing wall, and then implement the rescue as follows:

a. Position the ladder, with someone steadying the ladder.

b. Ascend to the climber and calmly assist him or her.

c. Keep the climber on belay until he or she is safely on the ground.

NOTE: Only highly qualified staff in extreme, critical circumstances should attempt a rescue by ascending a nearby rope using mechanical ascenders and a belayer. The ladder is convenient, is sturdier, and requires less extensive training.

If it is determined that a rescue *cannot be performed using the ladder,* the following steps should be taken:

Inform the building manager to call the nearest fire department.

Be sure to include the following information:

- WHERE the emergency is
- WHAT HAPPENED
- NUMBER OF PERSONS needing help
- CONDITION OF PERSON(S): conscious or unconscious; male or female; adult or child
- WHAT is being done for the victim

From *Climbing Walls: A Complete Guide* by Jim Stiehl and Tim B. Ramsey, 2005, Champaign, IL: Human Kinetics.

Climbing Wall Safety Notice

1. No climbing without the presence of an authorized climbing wall supervisor.

2. Climbers must use proper climbing technique at all times and must observe all safety rules associated with climbing on this wall.

3. Climbers must wear appropriate footwear and appropriate safety gear for climbing.

4. No more than _____ climbers may be on the wall at any time.

5. Climbers and observers will not engage in horseplay or other acts that may compromise the safety and well-being of themselves and others.

Climbers must have completed a participant agreement and safety policy contract before using the wall.

From *Climbing Walls: A Complete Guide* by Jim Stiehl and Tim B. Ramsey, 2005, Champaign, IL: Human Kinetics.

Climbing Wall Closed

Keep Off

CLIMBING WALL MISSION

To provide a challenging, enjoyable, yet safeguarded climbing experience that enhances both the academic and physical education of our students.

Appendix B

Resources

Associations/ Professional Support and Informational Sites

American Society for Testing and Materials (ASTM) www.astm.org

Association for Challenge Course Technology (ACCT) www.acctinfo.org

Association for Experiential Education (AEE) www.aee.org

Climbing Wall Association (CWA) www.climbingwallindustry.org

Climbing Wall Manufacturers Association UK (CWMA) www.cwma.co.uk

Comité Européen de Normalisation (CEN) www.cenorm.be / cenorm / index.htm

Competitive Climbing Rank www.ccrank.com

http:// directory.google.com / Top / Recreation / Climbing / Indoor /

Indoor Climbing www.indoorclimbing.com

International Mountaineering and Climbing Federation (UIAA) www.uiaa.ch and www.icc-info.org

Outdoor Network www.outdoornetwork.com

Professional Climbers Association (formerly ASCF) www.pcatour.com

Sporting Goods Manufacturers Association (SGMA) www.sgma.com

U.S. Consumer Product Safety Commission (CPSC) www.cpsc.gov

U.S. Gym Climbing List http:// rockclimb.org / gymsUS.html

Construction

Adventure Based Experiential Educators (ABEE), Inc. www.abeeinc.net

Building Climbing Walls: The Indoor Climber's Resource www.magma.ca / ~onsight / build.htm

ClimbUK Climbing Walls www.climbing.co.uk / features / walls1-1.htm

Edge Climbing Wall Systems www.edgewalls.com / homewall.htm

Home Climbing Walls FAQ www.tradgirl.com / climbing_faq / index.htm

Metolius Climbing How-To Guides www.metoliusclimbing.com / howto.htm

Planet-Climbing Training www.planetfear.com

Stone Age Climbing www.stoneageclimbing.com

Uncarved Block www.uncarvedblock.com.au

Vendors and Suppliers: Climbing Walls and Equipment

For updated listings, see http://dmoz.org/Recreation/Climbing/Gear_Manufacturers/Holds_and_Walls/

Adventure Hardware
    www.adventurehardware.com
Adventure Systems & Designs, Inc.
    www.adventuresystemsdesigns.com
Adventure Unlimited, Inc.
    www.adventureropes.com
Alpine Towers International
    www.alpinetowers.com
Bendcrete www.bendcrete.com
Entre Prises www.ep-usa.com
Gopher Sport www.gophersport.com
Grip-It Adventures
    www.giadventures.com
GR Climbing Holds www.grholds.com
Groperz Handholds www.traversewall.com/products/groperz_holds.shtml
High Performance Climbing Walls
    www.climbingwalls.net
High 5 www.high5adventure.org
Metolius Climbing Products
    www.metoliusclimbing.com
Nicros www.nicros.com
Petrogrips http://users.penn.com/~petro/
Project Adventure www.pa.org

Books and Articles

Hurni, M. 2003. *Coaching climbing: A complete program for coaching youth climbing for high performance and safety.* Guilford, CT: Falcon Books.

Hyder, M. 1999. Have your students climbing the walls: The growth of indoor climbing. *Journal of Physical Education, Recreation, and Dance* 70 (9): 32-36.

Leavitt, R. 1998. *Home climbing gyms: How to build and use.* Carbondale, CO: Climbing Magazine.

Lewis, S.P. and Cauthorn, D. 2000. *Climbing: From gym to crag.* Seattle: Mountaineers Books.

Long, J. 1992. *Face climbing.* Evergreen, CO: Chockstone Press.

Long, J. 1994. *Gym climb.* Evergreen, CO: Chockstone Press.

Luebben, C. 2001. *Knots for climbers* (2nd ed). Guilford, CT: Falcon Books.

Luebben, C. 2002. *Betty and the silver spider (or Welcome to gym climbing).* Boulder, CO: Sharp End Publishing.

Raleigh, D. 2003. *Knots and ropes for climbers.* Mechanicsburg, PA: Stackpole Books.

Rohnke, K. 1981. *High profile.* Hamilton, MA: Project Adventure.

Soles, C. 2004. *The outdoor knots book.* Seattle: Mountaineers Books.

Steffen, J. and Stiehl, J. 1995. Does your gym have six walls? *Journal of Physical Education, Recreation, and Dance* 66 (8): 43-47.

Urquhart, S. 1995. *Mock rock.* New Orleans: Paper Chase Press.

Climbing Magazines

Climbing Magazine www.climbing.com
Rock & Ice www.rockandice.com

glossary

anchored in (belayed)—Means by which a climber is secured while climbing.

arête—Outside corner of a climb (two corners meet, leaving a sharp ridge).

backswing—Losing grip and moving backward and away from the wall (see *pendulum*).

belayer—Person responsible for protecting the climber by managing the rope (taking up rope as a climber ascends the wall, and lowering the climber off the route).

bolt—Anchor placed in a drilled hole.

bucket—Large in-cut climbing hold that the climber can easily latch onto.

bulge—Portion of the wall that overhangs and then lessens in steepness.

buttress—Large face (flat area) that protrudes from a ridge or slope.

carabiner—Aluminum ring with spring-loaded snap gate, commonly used for attaching a belay device to the belayer's harness (locking carabiner); also used on each end of a quickdraw (nonlocking carabiner).

ceiling (also roof)—An overhang that juts out horizontally from the climbing wall.

chimney—Large crack that is big enough for a climber's body.

crimp—Small but positive sharp edge.

dihedral—Inside corner of a climb (angle created by two intersecting planes).

edge—Using the edge of a climbing shoe to stand on a small protrusion.

finger jamming—Wedging fingers into a crack to gain purchase (firm grip).

lead climbing—Type of climbing in which the climber uses protection anchors or quickdraws to safeguard a fall. If the climber falls, the protection or quickdraw and belayer will arrest the fall.

mantle shelf—Ledge requiring the climber to boost oneself by locking the elbows and bringing the feet up.

pendulum—Losing grip and moving sideways along the wall (see *backswing*).

pocket—Climbing hold into which a climber can place fingers and sometimes an entire hand.

protection anchor—Piece of equipment that is placed in a crack or clipped to a bolt hangar (using a quickdraw).

pumped—Slang for fatigued forearm muscles caused by buildup of lactic acid.

quickdraw—Short piece of sewn webbing with a carabiner attached to each end.

smear—Using the breadth of the climbing shoe sole to provide friction.

stem—To bridge oneself between two widely spaced holds.

traverse—To move sideways along the wall without gaining altitude.

references

Morris, G.S.D. and Stiehl, J. 1999. *Changing kids' games.* Champaign, IL: Human Kinetics.

Popke, M. 2003. Rock solid. *Athletic Business* (November): 54.

Powers, P. 1993. *NOLS wilderness mountaineering.* Mechanicsburg, PA: Stackpole Books.

Rohnke, K. and Grout, J. 1998. *Back pocket adventure.* Needham Heights, MA: Simon and Schuster.

index

Note: The italicized f following page numbers refers to figures.

about the authors

Jim Stiehl, PhD (right), is a professor in the School of Sport and Exercise Science at the University of Northern Colorado (UNC). Stiehl is a climbing instructor and challenge course director at UNC and has related experience as an instructor for the National Outdoor Leadership School.

Stiehl is former chair of the Council on Outdoor Education for the American Alliance for Health, Physical Education, Recreation and Dance (AAHPERD). He was named Scholar of the Year in 1993 for the Central District Association of HPERD and has received several research and writing excellence awards. He resides in Greeley, Colorado, with his wife, Julie, and enjoys backpacking and hiking, backcountry skiing and snowshoeing, and rock climbing and mountaineering in his leisure time.

Tim B. Ramsey, MSE (left), is a lecturer in the School of Sport and Exercise Science at the University of Northern Colorado (UNC). A longtime rock climber and mountaineer himself, Ramsey has taught rock-climbing activity classes at the college level since the late 1970s. As an outdoor and adventure educator, he also has taught rock-climbing fundamentals to a variety of populations, including college, high school, and adjudicated youths.

Ramsey, a member of AAHPERD, lives in Greeley, Colorado, with his wife, Melissa. He stays active outdoors through mountaineering, backcountry skiing, and hunting.